To my compatriots, I have no hesitation in saying that each one of us is as intimately attached to the soil of this beautiful country as are the famous jacaranda trees of Pretoria and the mimosa trees of the bushveld.

Each time one of us touches the soil of this land, we feel a sense of personal renewal. The national mood changes as the seasons change.

We are moved by a sense of joy and exhilaration when the grass turns green and the flowers bloom.

That spiritual and physical oneness we all share with this common homeland explains the depth of the pain we all carried in our hearts as we saw our country tear itself apart in a terrible conflict, and as we saw it spurned, outlawed and isolated by the peoples of the world, precisely because it has become the universal base of the pernicious ideology and practice of racism and racial oppression.

—Excerpt from Nelson Mandela's Inauguration Address, 1994

Daylight

HOMELANDS

Pieter de Vos

Cofounders: Taj Forer and Michael Itkoff
Art Director: Ursula Damm
Copy Editors: Nancy Hubbard, Barbara Richard

ISBN 978-1-942084-62-4

Printed by OFSET YAPIMEVI

Daylight Books
E-mail: info@daylightbooks.org
Web: www.daylightbooks.org

This book is dedicated to those who have made my homecoming possible.

***

To Donald for entrusting me with your friendship and your stories. To Colin and Denise for your enduring example of courage and justice in action. To Rachel for your support, encouragement, and your ongoing lessons in belonging. To Vera for your inspiration and guidance—and the gentle nudges that keep me on this path.

FOREWORD

—Leilani Farha, UN Special Rapporteur on the Right to Housing

Nearly one quarter of the world's urban population—close to 900 million people—live in informal settlements. 520 million are in Asia, over half of city dwellers in sub-Saharan Africa live in informal settlements, and in Latin America and the Caribbean the estimate is 21 percent.

The images in *Homelands* beautifully depict the dual reality of life in informal settlements experienced worldwide, where dignity and humanity are repeatedly affirmed amidst some of the most inhumane circumstances.

Informal settlements are a response to a formal system that is exclusionary. Individuals and families who migrate to cities for work or who are displaced from other neighborhoods often have no option but to create a subsidiary housing system to meet urgent needs that the formal housing system has failed to meet. Land at the margins of cities is often first settled informally, with informal businesses arising to respond to needs for water, sanitation, electricity, transportation, food, clothing, and other essentials. These settlements provide necessary housing for the laborers and service providers on whom cities rely, yet they are criminalized, denied services, face widespread discrimination, and are forced to pay exorbitant prices for basic necessities or go without.

Despite these disastrous outcomes of imposed informality, residents express a strong sense of community and home. Streets are named, houses numbered, residents' associations formed, community centers and schools built, social programs instituted, and shops and services established. In fact, for all their informality, these settlements are critical components of the economies of most major cities and are a main provider of housing in the global South and economies in transition.

From a human rights perspective, informal settlements have a dual nature. On the one hand, the scope and severity of the living conditions in informal settlements make this the most pervasive violation of human rights globally, the effects of state actions, inaction, and policies.

On the other hand, informal settlements are often an incredible accomplishment, a profound expression of individuals, families, and communities claiming their place and their right to housing. They are "habitats made by people," who are creating homes, culture, and community life in the most adverse circumstances. The act of claiming places in cities and constructing homes challenges spatial exclusion, the appropriation of land and property by the wealthy for no purpose but speculation, the colonization of Indigenous territories and attempts by authorities to render entire communities invisible by not recognizing them. In response informal settlements are statements: "We are here" and "We will not disappear."

The breathtaking photographs by Pieter de Vos demonstrate how human beings cling to their dignity and find its expression in a myriad of ways: through art, political action, sports, and the assertion of home. *Homelands* is a cry to those of us living comfortably, to governments, to those with power and influence, that while conditions in informal settlements are not acceptable, there is something very special to preserve there.

INTRODUCTION

—Pieter de Vos

No one may be evicted from their home or have their home demolished, without an order of court made after considering all the relevant circumstances. No legislation may permit arbitrary evictions.

— Section 26(3) of the Constitution of South Africa

This book traces its origins to South Africa—the country of my birth and the country where I have been undertaking narrative and documentary work since 2012. The object of my affection is Woodlane Village, an informal settlement located in the affluent suburb of Moreleta Park, Pretoria.

I was drawn to the Village because of its unique history. It was created as a temporary settlement in 2009, following years of advocacy and legal battles by Colin and Denise Dredge—a husband and wife who intervened as an act of faith on behalf of homeless individuals squatting on vacant land near Woodlands Boulevard Mall, the self-proclaimed fashion capital of Pretoria. The Dredges and the nonprofit organization they founded in 2003, Tswelopele Step by Step, directed their initial efforts to improve the living conditions of the squatters, but they were eventually drawn to defend the squatters' human rights in the face of repeated harassment by the metro police.

I wanted to understand how people experience home and belonging in a community that straddles the tension between social inclusion and exclusion. How do personal journeys, memories, and imaginations shape these concepts? How do the experiences of migration from countryside to town or from country to country influence one's sense of place? What does it mean to live in an informal settlement sanctified by court order in a locality where countervailing forces oppose one's presence and where impulses toward place-making are at odds with narratives of otherness?

What follows is the product of this homecoming. It is an attempt to make sense of the experiences of "home" and "belonging" through the stories we tell about our lives and the places we live. At the heart of this book are the interlocking and cross-cutting narratives of Donald Banda along with my photographs as we inquire about these concepts and our common connection to South Africa. As a former South African of Afrikaner ancestry, the mixing of spirits and stories that occurred across the racial divide was profound and took us into uncharted territory.

This book is a testament to the changes that are possible when we live alongside others — when we cross the threshold between "us" and "them".

Donald was born in South Africa, although he traces his ancestry to Malawi. He grew up in Pretoria East close to where the informal settlement is situated. He was arrested for the first time in 1974 and eventually spent two decades behind bars. In 1997, he was released to face a new life in postapartheid South Africa—a transformed man in a transformed country. Donald has a stand in Woodlane Village and has lived in the community since its establishment. In late 2017, he relocated with his wife, Rose, to another informal settlement near the township of Mamelodi. He is employed as a workhand at the NG Moreleta Church and does tailoring on the side. Donald is the former chair of the executive committee of the Village. Our relationship developed as I sat with him while he repaired clothing in the late afternoons.

Since 2012, I have spent countless hours in conversation with him and others in Woodlane Village and beyond. Exchanges occurred in a variety of settings including around campfires, on the streets, on the football pitch, in automobiles, in shacks where our warm breath condensed on cold metal roofs, and in the bustling townships around Pretoria. They spoke of shadow lives. In some cases, the stories were confessional in nature, disclosing a multitude of struggles. Other times, they were self-aggrandizing, as individuals spoke of past accomplishments or of their prowess in navigating the dog-eat-dog world of South Africa. There were stories of grief and loss; stories of hopes and dreams; stories of resignation and defeat; and stories of rage and defiance.

For the first two years, I focused exclusively on relationship-building and collecting stories. I recorded and transcribed hundreds of hours of conversations to produce narrative accounts, which represent the sensitive interweaving of discursive fragments. Donald's narrative account, along with those of three other men who live in the settlement, formed the basis for a doctoral dissertation in anthropology (de Vos, 2014).

The process of producing the narrative accounts was collaborative with informed consent. Each stage of the storytelling process was negotiated, emerging stories were reviewed and redrafted, and the final product was bound and given to all participants.

This book contains an abridged version of the account of home and belonging that Donald shared over an extended period of time. The oral history is a reconstruction—my attempt to convey his perspectives and his voice in a manner that is authentic, while maintaining readability. It is written in a way that evokes the sporadic and fluid ways in which he speaks about his life.

Although his story is situated within Woodlane Village, it speaks to the larger experience of being human. In this way, it offers insights of universal relevance, while also addressing the unique realities of postapartheid South Africa.

In 2015, I started taking photographs to document Donald's life. Initially, the epicenter of my photography work was his compound in the settlement. His stand included a courtyard surrounded by a bamboo fence where he met neighbors and entertained guests. The courtyard featured a fire pit and a sitting area made of inlaid bricks in a circular pattern. Music was often playing in this space. Eventually, my field of view expanded as I was introduced to his family and friends in the surrounding townships. A larger web of relations to other home-places was revealed.

The photographs in this book trace a similar arc. They start by documenting everyday life in the informal settlement. They then shift to the intimate space of Donald's compound before moving on to chronicle encounters in the communities of Winterveld, Mamelodi, Soshanguve, and KwaMhlanga.

TRAJECTORIES OF HOME

During my time in the informal settlement, it has become apparent to me that home and belonging are slippery concepts. In a world shaped by globalization and migration, these notions are ambiguous as we "move astride, betwixt and between old and new homes" (Ralph, 2009: 184). Sometimes, Donald described home as a place of birth. Other times, he used the concepts metaphorically to describe the trajectory of his experiences. Often his reflections on home and belonging veered from recollections of the past to present-day concerns about the conditions in the camp to free-flowing explorations of life and selfhood, touching on his origins and the changing world.

Donald provides contradictory assessments of life in Woodlane Village, describing the environment as familiar yet alien; organized yet unruly; a community as well as a "no-man's-land." The betwixt and between nature of Woodlane Village compels ambivalent attachments and distributed efforts to place-make. The specter of impermanence and change hangs over the community. Economic realities and uncertainties induce the hedging of bets and the straddling of localities.

Donald traces his childhood to Pretoria East. Home is envisioned as a place of ancestral roots, a place where the umbilical cords of his predecessors were planted at birth, a place where his relatives are buried in soil that has since been built over. As Donald told me during a drive through Moreleta Park:

> *Look around you, Pieter. It grows to be this town where I don't even know which street to go, but I was born here. Because the jungle, it just crossed that way and that way and that way. Now it is a town, but I don't know which street is which . . . because it was planned by somebody who didn't even know what the jungle was.*

He references a time before the countryside became the city. These imaginaries of home evoke nostalgia, speaking of bygone traditions and values. He recalls memories of a time when the cycles of life and death were tied to the same land—where the deceased were wrapped in cowhide and interred in the very ground upon which they were born. Rural life is described as peaceful and neighborly in comparison to the hard-edged anonymity of the city.

Donald describes the dislocations he has experienced. He speaks of love and loss and of the yearning to live in community with others despite the forces tearing relationships apart. These disruptions are set against the urbanization of the land, the transformation of farms into suburbs, and the displacement of people from Pretoria East to the *lokasies*, the euphemistic term for the impoverished black settlements that surround Pretoria. As Donald observes:

> *"We ran out here to make a life. I mean there is no place like home. But if home no longer feels like home, we are lost. We are a lost generation."*

His stories reveal the sociocultural, political, and spatial dimensions of home and belonging. The legacy of apartheid and the rise of neoliberalism in South Africa have created and sustained polarizations, leading to contrasts and displacements. Informal settlements are a ubiquitous feature of the country as the poor occupy land close to sources of employment. The flow of immigrants and refugees from other African countries seeking economic opportunities in South Africa has also exacerbated housing challenges. There are approximately 279,000 shacks in Pretoria distributed among 66 informal settlements (Housing Development Agency, 2013b). Woodlane Village is small example of a much larger dynamic. As Donald says:

> *Here, you will find children who have been raised in holes in the jungle. When they say "home," they are referring to this place. And when this land is turned into a suburb and they no longer have a home, they will dig another hole in another jungle. That's how people live.*

There is unsettledness in his accounts of home and belonging, hinting at the fragility and conditionality of these concepts. There are gaps and empty spaces. Stories begin and end, sometimes without resolution. There are mysteries, hints, and provocations. Queries are made and only partially answered. This is suggestive of how we experience life—not as a clean and coherent flow of events, but as the back-and-forth movement between immediate perception, memory, and imagination. The account mirrors the way in which stories are told and lived—the monologues, the confessions, the fits and starts, the substance and the minutia, the segues, the repetitions and the contradictions, the calls and the responses.

HOMECOMINGS

During my time in Woodlane Village, my experience of home was also in flux. My story and sense of belonging changed over time. Strangers became friends. The boundary between "self" and "other" collapsed. One cannot be privy to the intimacies of people's experiences without being reoriented to one's own story and to the existential and moral questions posed by the human condition.

In many ways, my homecoming involved a movement in two directions. On one hand, I experienced a regressive "holding on" to memories of relationships and localities imbued with emotional significance. On the other hand, I also underwent a progressive "letting go" of these attachments: the acceptance of change and the willingness to rediscover the self and home in the present (Joannidis, 2012).

My homecoming forced me to confront my own experiences of dislocation. I was born in Bloemfontein in 1970 and my roots can be traced back to the first Dutch settlers who came to the country in the 1650s. My extended family is firmly planted in South Africa, although a handful of my relatives have moved to Canada, Australia, and the United States.

My parents were some of the first members of my family to leave South Africa, having decided to pack up their children to escape what they saw as the impending social and moral collapse of the country. It is a decision that came with sacrifice. For my parents, the cost was the loss of a previous life, the separation from family and friends, and the struggle to gain an economic foothold in Canada. I paid the price of being set adrift in the liminal space between two societies—to grow up being of both places, but not fully belonging to either.

It turned out that they acted with prescience. The Soweto Uprising occurred three months after our departure. On June 16, 1976, children from several Sowetan schools began protesting the introduction of Afrikaans as the language of instruction. In the resulting aftermath and riots, buildings and vehicles were burned, stones were thrown, police bullets shattered young bodies, and Hector Pieterson was shot dead at twelve years of age. According to conservative estimates, 294 people were killed during the first three months of the protests, but accounts of the events are confusing and contradictory. History offers no simple answers, but it is clear a line had been crossed on that day (Pohlandt-McCormick, 2005).

Our lives are full of moments where we are challenged to see our individual stories as part of a larger unfolding narrative. My parents' decision to emigrate is one such instance. It set a new direction for our lives. My paternal grandfather's decision to break away from the Nederduitse Gereformeerde Kerk (NGK) to start his own congregation in 1944 is another such moment.

My grandfather was a former minister in the NGK who opposed what he considered to be the theological perversions within the institution. At the time, both the NGK and the government were controlled by the Broederbond, a secret society of Afrikaner nationalists who were driven by the belief that the Afrikaner *volk* had been planted in the country by God's hand and they were destined to remain there as a nation (Goldberg, 2009). Under the Broederbond, the NGK became a political instrument. The traditional Calvinism of the Afrikaners combined with a quest for political sovereignty to produce the Christian nationalism that dominated South Africa from 1948 to 1994 (Davies, 2009). The collusion of church and state provided the vehicle for Afrikaner independence and for the realization of apartheid in 1948 (Van der Merwe, 2009).

My grandfather became an outspoken critic of both the corruption in the church and of the Broederbond's role in politics and religion. As a consequence, he was under police protection because of threats against his life. He died in 1971, before I was able to know him and fully understand his story. This is one of the many gaps that comes from growing up away from extended family.

I spent most of my adolescence wrestling with the conflicting emotions that accompanied my immigration experience. Growing up in Canada during the late 1980s, I was often embarrassed of my association with South Africa. It was during this period of time that international pressure was being exerted on the country to abolish apartheid. Although I was ashamed of my homeland's discriminatory policies, I was also aware of the hypocrisy that underlay Canada's opposition. Canada's historic treatment of its Aboriginal population has been equally atrocious. We have also promoted a polarized society by creating Indian reserves, by classifying Indigenous Peoples along race lines, by denying them the right to vote until 1960, and by attempting to forcibly assimilate them through a church- and state-sanctioned policy of residential schooling.

South Africa has always hovered in the background, a reminder that I come from elsewhere. My immigration to Canada and subsequent return visits to South Africa coincide with turning points in the country's history: the Soweto Uprising in 1976, the release of Nelson Mandela from Robben Island in 1990, the democratic transition in 1993 leading to the first general election in 1994, the rise of Julius Malema in 2011, the Marikana massacre in 2012, the rapid decline of the African National Congress (ANC) under President Jacob Zuma in 2016 and 2017.

But the most significant turning point in my personal history with South Africa occurred when I met Donald. My perspective on my homeland shape-shifted. Anger and grief morphed into serenity. At times, the swings were so dramatic that previous perspectives and insights seemed alien to me—as if they emerged from another life. Somewhere along the line, I fell in love with the country of my birth and reclaimed a sense of belonging that transcends the complications of distance, history, and race.

As Donald shared with me, "there is a story in our story," alluding to the obligations, respect, and trust that form the foundation of our relationship. Our lives are interwoven—and in the warp and weft of our commitments and our shared experiences we have fashioned the enduring fabric of friendship. Over the past seven years, we have grieved the losses of loved ones together and celebrated the emergence of new unions. When I wed in 2014, I took Rachel to meet them and Donald accompanied us on our honeymoon. In 2015, I was a signatory to Donald's marriage to Rose. In 2017, I helped Donald and Rose secure a foothold in Solomon Mahlangu Village, an informal settlement near Mamelodi, where they have established a new home. As Donald says, "We have grown attached to this guy. And we never asked to be. Now, we are kind of like a rope, triple-woven."

The shift in our relationship occurred when we visited his family and friends in the townships. It was an opportunity to journey together, to share adventures outside the confines of the settlement, to go where he calls home. In hindsight, there was nothing remarkable about the form and content of our encounters. They were rather ordinary. There were the daily conversations in Woodlane Village spanning the bone-rattling cold of July and the torrid heat of late October. There were the long commutes to the townships and the stops along the way to run errands. There was the gridlock. The intersections and the speed bumps. There were the countless introductions to family and friends, the halting conversations and the polite smiles. The gestures of hospitality: a cold drink, a seat in the shade, the pap burning our fingertips. There were the moments of laughter, boredom, and fatigue. And on the return journeys, there were the road stories, the jokes, and the recollections of the sights seen and the people met.

They were mundane encounters. The only notable thing is that they happened.

FLASHBACKS AND SNAPSHOTS

It is a Monday evening in mid-August 2011, the end of a winter day in Pretoria (City of Tshwane Metropolitan Municipality). The sun hovers low in the sky, preparing to plunge below the horizon. Plumes of smoke rise from shacks as residents of Woodlane Village prepare meals and seek heat over wood fires. The temperature has dropped to around 2 degrees Celsius (35 degrees Fahrenheit)—frigid enough that even the delegation of Canadian academics is finding it uncomfortable. We are here on a site visit as part of a bilateral exchange with South African researchers to compare and contrast homelessness between the two countries.

The informal settlement spreads over eight hectares of land on the corner of De Villebois Mareuil and Garsfontein roads near the exclusive Woodhill Golf Estate. It sits immediately adjacent to a gargantuan Dutch Reformed Church with a congregation of more than 7,000 people.

Woodlane Village comprises 846 households representing around 3,000 people from Zimbabwe, Lesotho, Mozambique, and provinces in South Africa. Most of the residents are political and economic migrants.

The informal settlement is contested. It was created as a temporary camp in 2009 following a protracted and acrimonious series of court cases. For some residents, the place is a refuge, a green pasture. For others, it is a stop of last resort, a no-man's-land. The Village is called "Plastic View" by the surrounding homeowners who describe the place as a hotbed of crime and pestilence—and oppose integration and community-building efforts.

Tshwane Metropolitan Municipality provides potable water and latrines to the Village. In addition, the area is fenced off and guards are posted at the entrances of the settlement as a measure of security and as a strategy to contain the camp's growth. The fence keeps others out and the residents in.

I am in a confluence of narratives that flow in and out of Woodlane Village: the stories of the residents who live here and their experiences of migration, home, and belonging; the stories of those who fought to keep them out of Moreleta Park; the stories of those who have fought to keep them in; the stories of my family and our history; the stories of South Africa as it makes sense of its past and charts an uncertain course to the future.

The Village is a crucible for many of the pressures South Africa is experiencing around land, migration, housing, the polarization of classes and the entrenchment of an economic form of segregation, the role of the church and state in shaping the overlapping stories of place and nation, and the larger frame of globalization that is reconfiguring the relationships between countries and shifting economic and political structures.

It is hard to imagine that people here spend the bitter cold in shelters made of little more than plastic tarps, recycled cardboard, scraps of plywood, and zinc. Yet, despite the makeshift construction of the buildings, the settlement has an orderly feel. There is a sense of care and pride. The shacks are organized in rows separated by wide lanes that permit easy access for motorized vehicles and also serve as fire-breaks. Some of the properties are set up as grocery stores and spaza shops. Others have gardens. On warmer days, colorful laundry hangs from clotheslines and children play in the dirt roads between shacks. But on a miserable winter day like this one, people hunker down to avoid the wind that cuts across the open fields, ripping at the tarpaulins.

I feel the irresistible urge to wander the camp by myself—to dive into the sensory stream of this place without the voiceover and surveillance of a tour guide. It is the same impulse that has compelled me over the years to document a range of topics photographically, including homelessness and poverty, the community experience of HIV/AIDS, gentrification, and the reconstruction efforts in Haiti after the earthquake there.

I break away from my colleagues to explore the camp on my own, searching for visual signs and symbols to help me understand this locality. My camera is a tool I use to explore and make sense of the world. It allows me to isolate moments of reflection in currents of experience.

I spot a Dickies canvas shoe hanging from barbed wire—a hint of the new economic order where a shoe made by an American company incorporated in 1922 and popularized by the hip-hop scene in the 1990s can become part of a fence in South Africa in 2011. The enormous Dutch Reformed Church sits in the near distance, a physical and metaphorical backdrop to the human drama that unfolds before it. I shift to juxtapose the building against the shacks in the foreground.

The movement of person and camera continues as I see, compose, and reflect on images both inside and out the frame. Being in places involves immersion in the sights, sounds, smells, and atmosphere of a locale, and contemplation about the traces of thought, imagination, and investment that have influenced their physical and metaphorical construction over time: the laundry blowing in the winter wind, the fire-breaks, the gardens and spaza shops, the residents cooking salted fish, the parade of foreigners on tours to see how the "other side" lives, the fence that defines a physical boundary between inclusion and exclusion.

Stories unfold as the external world resonates with our inner worlds; as sensory perceptions trigger memories and imaginations; and as individual histories connect to the larger histories of place, evoking questions of home and belonging.

At the edge of every frame is a borderland. It is a terrain where internal and external ways of knowing rub against each other. It is a landscape of shifting liminal spaces where the interplay of subject and object blur the convenient dichotomies we use to situate ourselves in the world. It is an intersubjective territory where our singular lives are simultaneously part of a commonality—individual yet part of the whole.

REFERENCES

Davies, Rebecca. *Afrikaners in the New South Africa: Identity Politics in a Globalized Economy* (London and New York: Tauris Academic Studies, 2009).

de Vos, Pieter Francois. *Homelands: A Narrative Inquiry into Home and Belonging in an Informal Settlement in South Africa* (doctoral dissertation, 2014), Edmonton, Alberta. Retrieved from: https://era.library.ualberta.ca/items/e3edb899-4276-415b-875d-cef1eae58480

Goldberg, David Theo. *The Threat of Race: Reflections on Racial Neoliberalism.* (Malden, Oxford and Victoria: Wiley-Blackwell, 2009).

Housing Development Agency. *South Africa: Informal Settlements Status in Gauteng* (2013). Downloaded from: http://www.thehda.co.za/resources/entry/informal-settlement-status-in-gauteng-2013

Joannidis, Christo. "Homecoming." *International Forum of Psychcanalysis,* (2012), 22(3): 133-141.

Pohlandt-McCormick, Helena. *"I Saw a Nightmare..." Doing Violence to Memory: The Soweto Uprising, June 16, 1976* (Columbia University Press, 2005).

Ralph, David. "Home Is Where the Heart Is? Understandings of 'Home' Among Irish-born Return Migrants from the United States" 2009. *Irish Studies Review* 17(2): 183–200.

Van der Merwe, Jan. *An Anthropological Perspective on Afrikaner Narrative and Myths* (2009). *Identity, Culture & Politics: An Afro-Asian Dialogue* 10(1): 30–50.

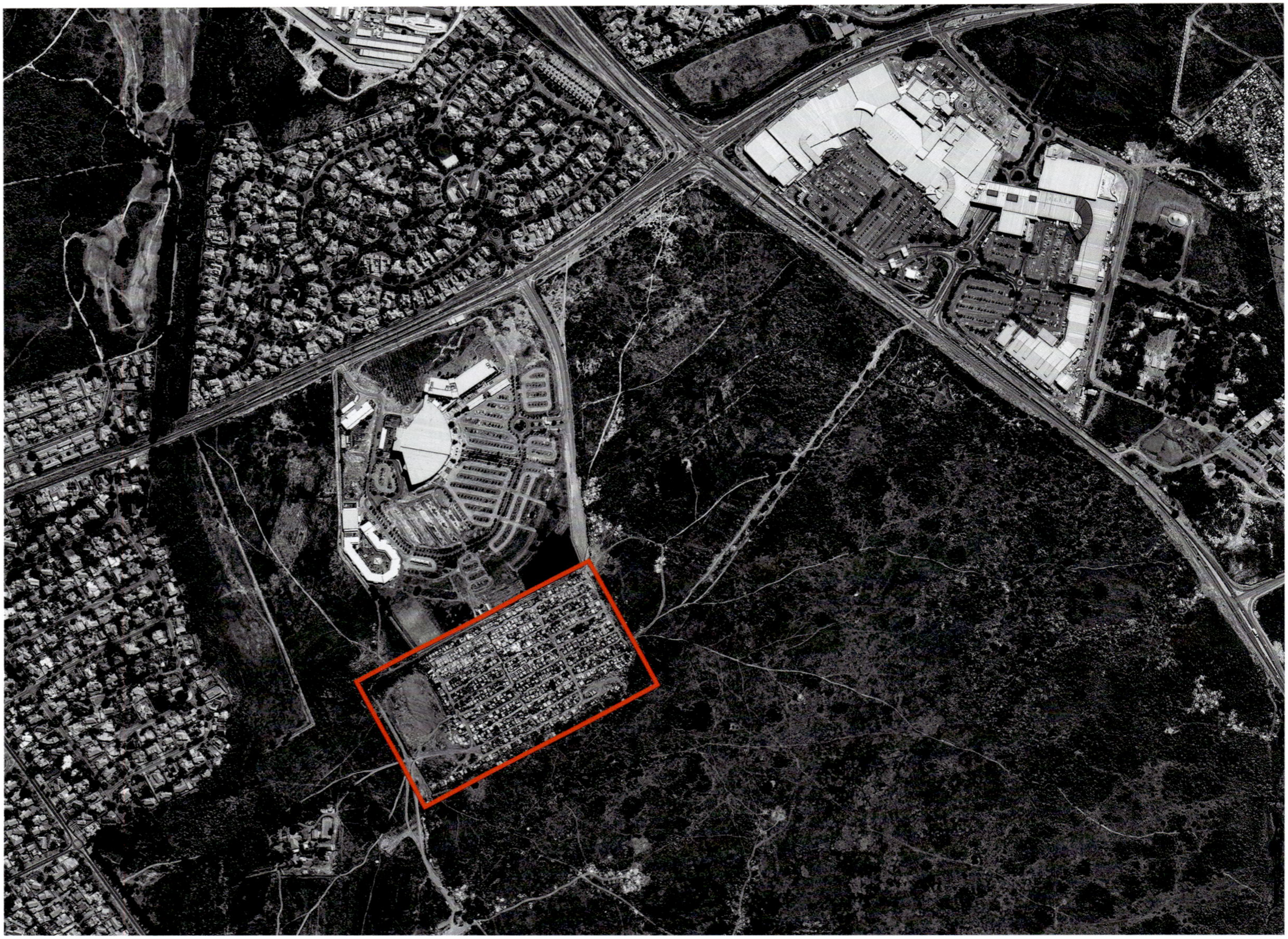

Satellite image of Woodlane Village (red square) taken on March 14, 2018. The pie-shaped building above the settlement is NG Moreleta Church. The shopping complex in the upper right-hand corner of the photo is Woodlands Boulevard Mall. (Image © 2018 DigitalGlobe, Inc.)

A BRIEF HISTORY OF WOODLANE VILLAGE

2004

- People start occupying vacant land in the suburb of Moreleta Park near Woodlands Boulevard Mall. Many are refugees fleeing the economic and political meltdown in Zimbabwe.
- The Garsfontein Police and security personnel, stoked by complaints from local homeowners and businesses, attempt to drive out the squatters. Numerous instances of property destruction and violence (including shootings) are perpetrated against the squatters.
- Tswelopele Step by Step (a local NGO) responds to improve the living conditions of the squatters, but is eventually called to address escalating violations of human rights.

2006

- Tshwane Metropolitan Council, the police, and the Department of Home Affairs mount two raids to destroy the belongings of the squatters. In one of these, the municipality claims it was an operation to "eradicate alien vegetation," while the police assert it was a "crime-fighting effort." Tswelopele engages Impact Litigation Lawyers to represent the people. Later Lawyers for Human Rights (NGO) takes the case to the Supreme Court of Appeal.

2007

- A landmark ruling by the Supreme Court of Appeal on May 30 determines the eviction of the squatters by Tshwane Metro Council is illegal and that the government agencies are responsible for rebuilding the structures demolished in the raids.
- Safety and Security Minister Charles Nqakula does not comply with this order. Police and security personnel raze fifty more shacks in the early morning of August 16 in defiance of the interdict.
- In a subsequent legal case on August 29, Adriaan Vorster of Impact Litigation Lawyers argues that: "If the police could demolish shacks at 4 in the morning then surely they could rebuild them at 4 in the morning."
- The Pretoria High Court holds Minister Nqakula in contempt of court and issues a warrant for his arrest. A fine of R10,000 is also imposed on him. The Court orders the police to replace the torched shacks within twelve hours.
- The shacks are rebuilt and Minister Nqakula avoids arrest.

2008

- A group of local homeowners' associations attempt to obtain a lawful eviction of the squatters. In court, Tshwane Metro claims it cannot provide a viable alternative area for the squatters to live.
- The Court compels the municipality to establish a temporary settlement for the squatters within a demarcated area in Moreleta Park and to devise a relocation plan for the residents in the camp.

2009

- The people start moving into the demarcated area over the Easter weekend. They comply peacefully with the court order and the Tshwane officials who allocate the stands. No security forces are required to induce the move. It takes until September 2009 for everyone to relocate as they have to disassemble their shacks by hand and move all of their building materials and possessions by foot.

2015

- In violation of the court order, the municipality attempts to auction off the land where Woodlane Village is situatec. Lawyers for Human Rights blocks the attempt in court.

2016

- In the early morning of July 3, a fire destroys 200 shacks and kills five people in Woodlane Village. The catastrophe makes international news. In testimony to a remarkable shift in societal attitudes, people near and far rally to assist in providing food, clothing, blankets, and even building materials for those affected by the blaze.

EXCERPT FROM LEGAL JUDGEMENT
Supreme Court of Appeal of South Africa

Tswelopele Non-Profit Organization v City of Tshwane Metropolitan Municipality [2007] SCA 70 (RSA)

1. In the early hours of Friday morning 31 March 2006, about one hundred persons were evicted from their homes on a vacant piece of land in the Pretoria suburb of Garsfontein. Officials from three governmental agencies in a joint operation expelled them from the rudimentary shelters they had erected. The pieces of plastic and other waste materials they had salvaged from surrounding building sites to construct their homes were put to the torch. Many of their belongings were destroyed. Sixteen immigrants without South African documentation were arrested and later deported.

2. The operation was carried out by officials from the nature conservation division of the Tshwane metropolitan municipality (Tshwane) (first respondent), the immigration control office of the Department of Home Affairs (Home Affairs) (second respondent), and the South African Police Services (SAPS) (third respondent), accompanied by members of the Garsfontein community policing forum. Even though the Constitution provides that "No one may be evicted from their home, or have their home demolished, without an order of court made after considering all the relevant circumstances," and even though the Prevention of Illegal Eviction from and Unlawful Occupation of Land Act 19 of 1998 ("PIE") decrees that "No person may evict an unlawful occupier except on the authority of an order of a competent court," there was no court order. The eviction violated the law and the Constitution.

3. This led the first appellant—a registered non-profit organization committed to the upliftment of homeless and destitute people in the Moreleta Park area (Tswelopele "Progress")—to bring an urgent application ten days later in the Pretoria High Court. Twenty-three named residents who had been evicted (the occupiers) joined the proceedings as applicants. In the founding affidavit, Tswelopele's treasurer, Mr. Colin Wilfred Dredge, a chartered accountant living in Moreleta Park (which borders on Garsfontein), described what he saw after receiving a call from distressed occupiers. Dwellings in which they had been living peaceably for at least eighteen months had been destroyed. In the wake of the police, Tshwane employees were burning shacks and cutting down trees. When challenged, officials from all three government agencies refused to show him authorization under a court order. Indeed, he says, he was threatened with arrest for obstructing the police in the execution of their duties.

4. In the face of this, Tswelopele sought an order directing the three respondents to restore the possession of the occupiers before all else (ante omnia), and in the interim to provide them with temporary shelter. The notice of motion also sought costs and further or alternative relief. The founding affidavit couched its claim for relief under the common law mandament van spolie: but it also expressly invoked the occupiers' procedural protections under PIE and their rights under sections 25 and 26(3) of the Bill of Rights.

5. In answer, Tshwane protested that its officials were there merely "to eradicate alien vegetation" (even while admitting

that its nature conservation division was not responsible for the site), and that they did so believing that the police "were acting lawfully." Home Affairs said it participated solely "to identify non-documented illegal immigrants." The Garsfontein police station acting commander, senior superintendent John Tinyiko Masia—who admitted planning the action with the other governmental agencies—described it as but a "crime fighting operation." He and Home Affairs (though contradicted in this by Tshwane's deponent) denied that any dwellings were destroyed or dwellers evicted. Instead, they said, the occupiers left "voluntarily," leaving their waste materials behind to be cleared.

.
.
.

15. That the wanton destruction of the occupiers' dwellings violated the Constitution was not disputed. What must be owned is how far-reaching and damaging the breach was. The governmental agencies violated not merely the fundamental warrant against unauthorized eviction, but (given the implicit menace with which the eviction was carried out) the occupiers' right to personal security and their right to privacy. It infringed not only the occupiers' property rights in their materials and belongings, but trampled on their feelings and affronted their social standing. For to be hounded unheralded from the privacy and shelter of one's home, even in the most reduced circumstances, is a painful and humiliating indignity.

16. And it is not for nothing that the constitutional entrenchment of the right to dignity emphasizes that "everyone" has inherent dignity, which must be respected and protected. Historically, police actions against the most vulnerable in this country had a distinctive racial trajectory: white police abusing blacks. The racial element may have disappeared, but what has not changed is the exposure of the most vulnerable in society to police power and their vulnerability to its abuse. Reading comparable case reports from the decades preceding these events, it is impossible not to endorse appellant's counsel's submission that in its lack of respect for the poor and the vulnerable, and in the official hubris displayed, what happened displays a repetition of the worst of the pre-constitutional past.

"Informal settlement" means one shack or more constructed on land, with or without the consent of the owner of the land or the person in charge of the land.

— City of Tshwane Metropolitan Municipality By-laws Relating to the Management and Control of Informal Settlements

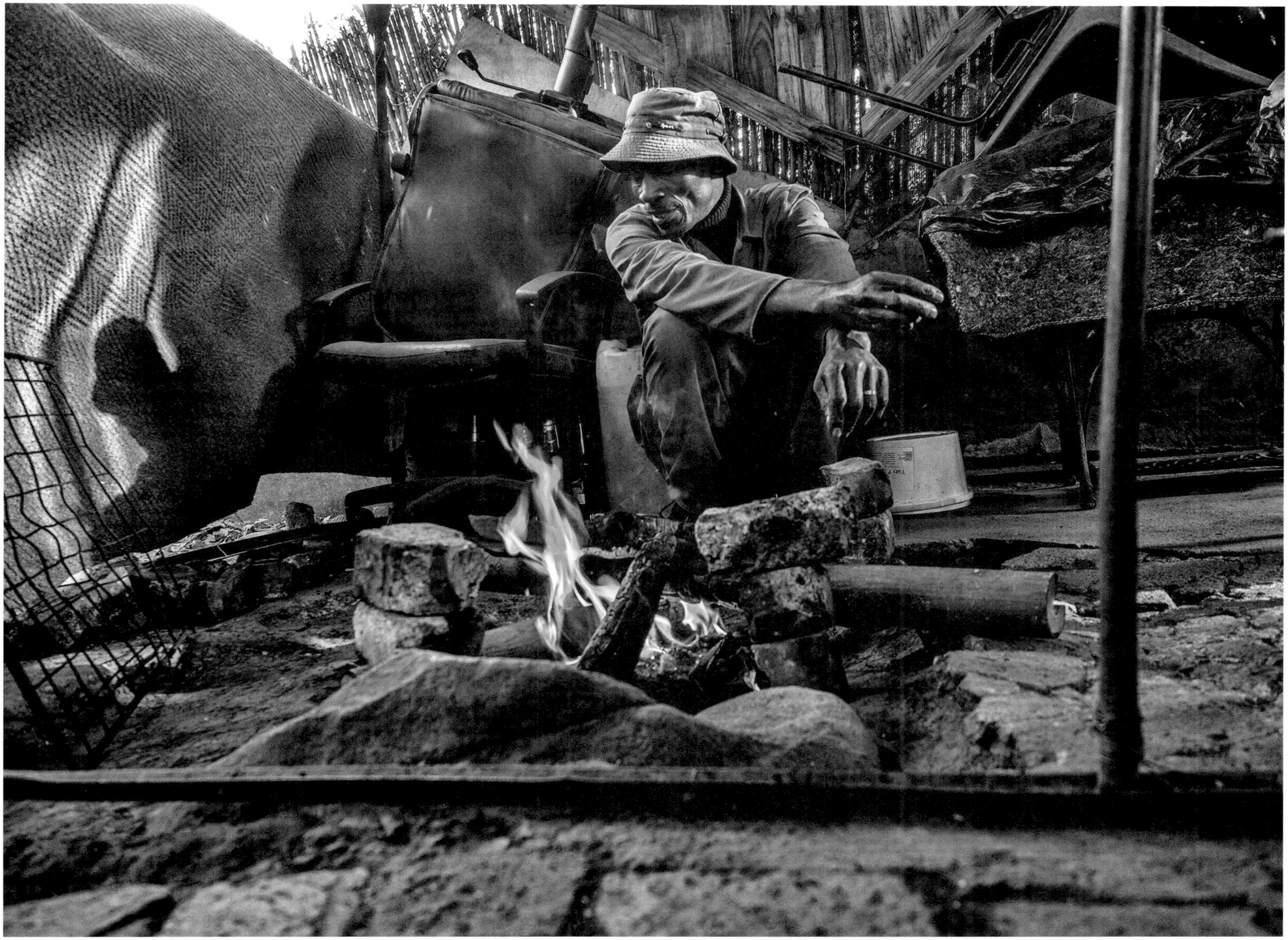

Donald Banda warms himself next to a fire on a cold August night in 2016

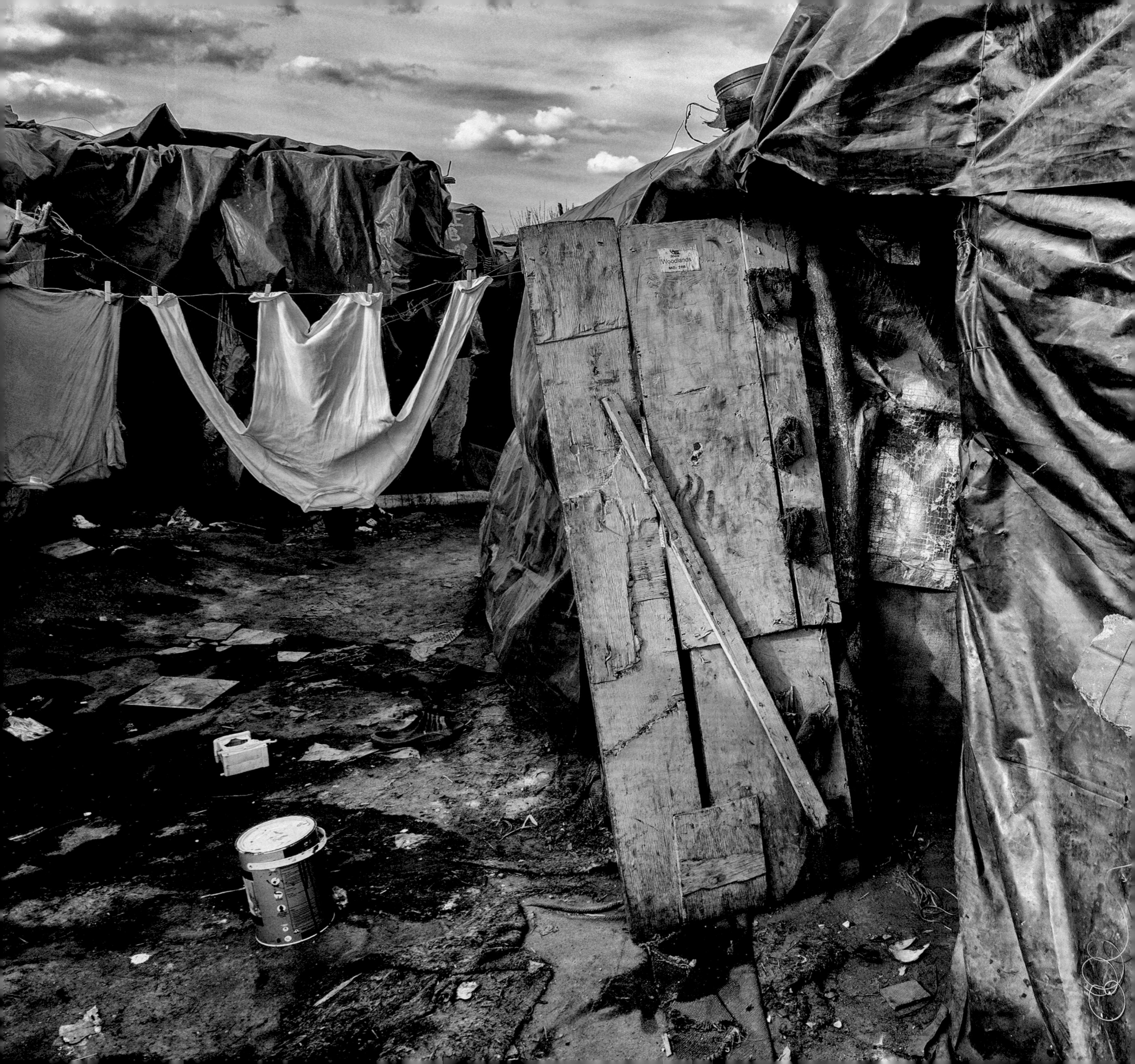
Woodlands

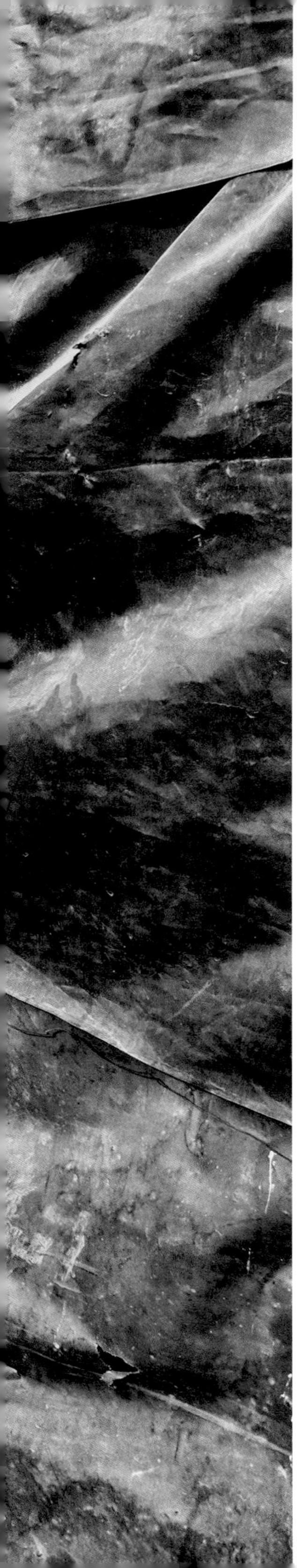

Laundry spans the divide
between two shacks
in Woodlane Village
(August 2015)

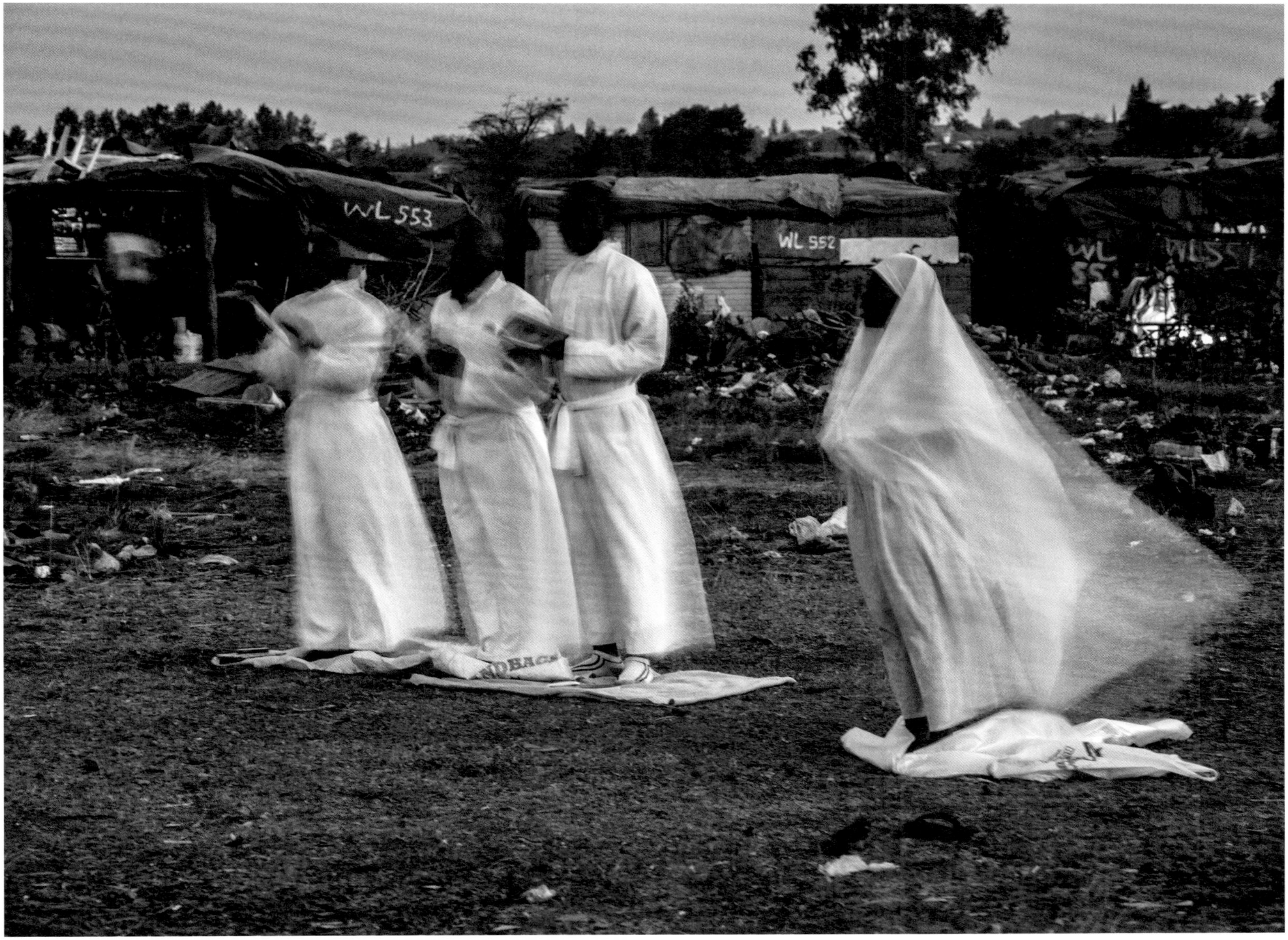

Evening gospel #1 (September 2017)

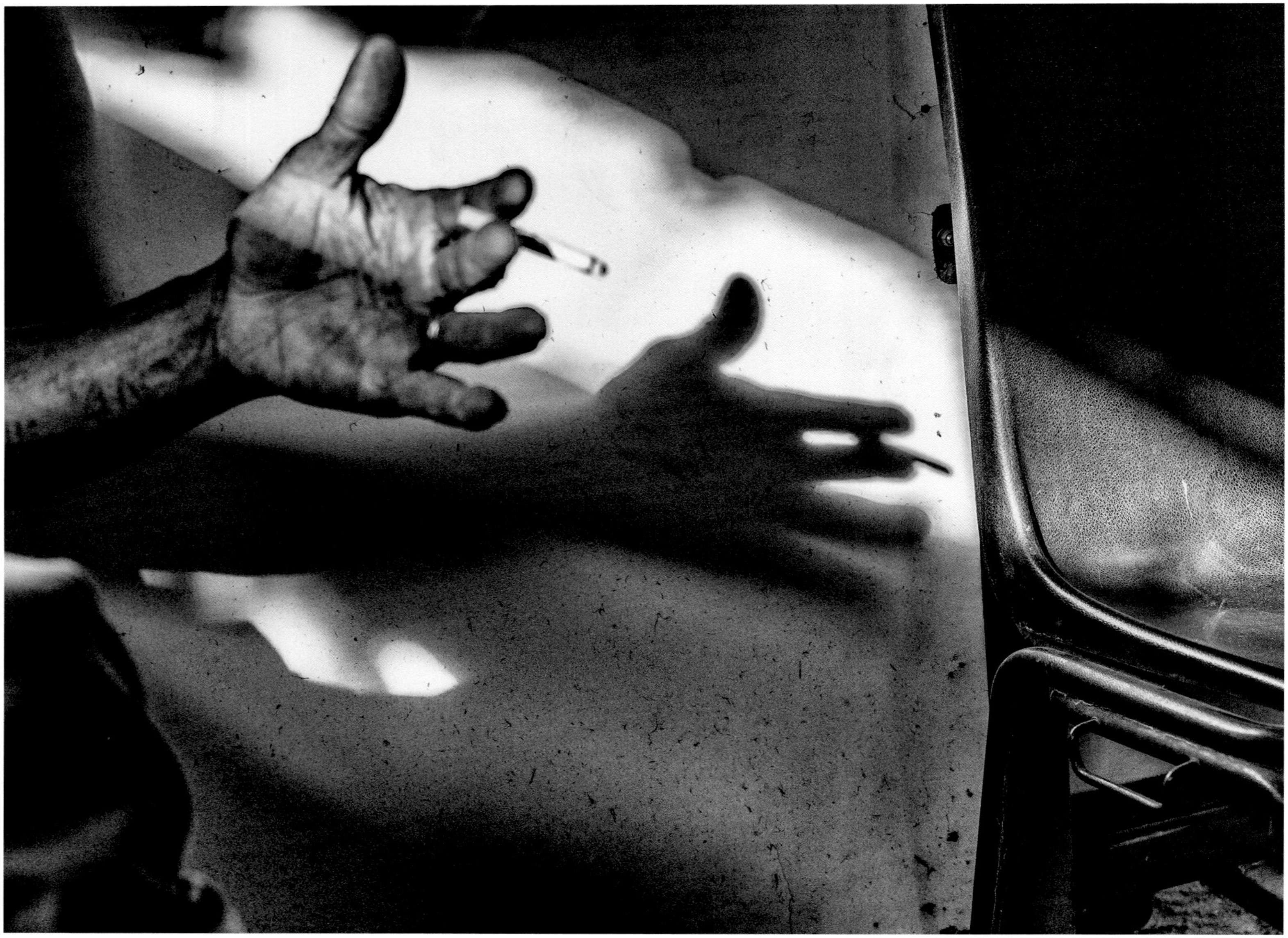

The shadow of Donald's hand (September 2017)

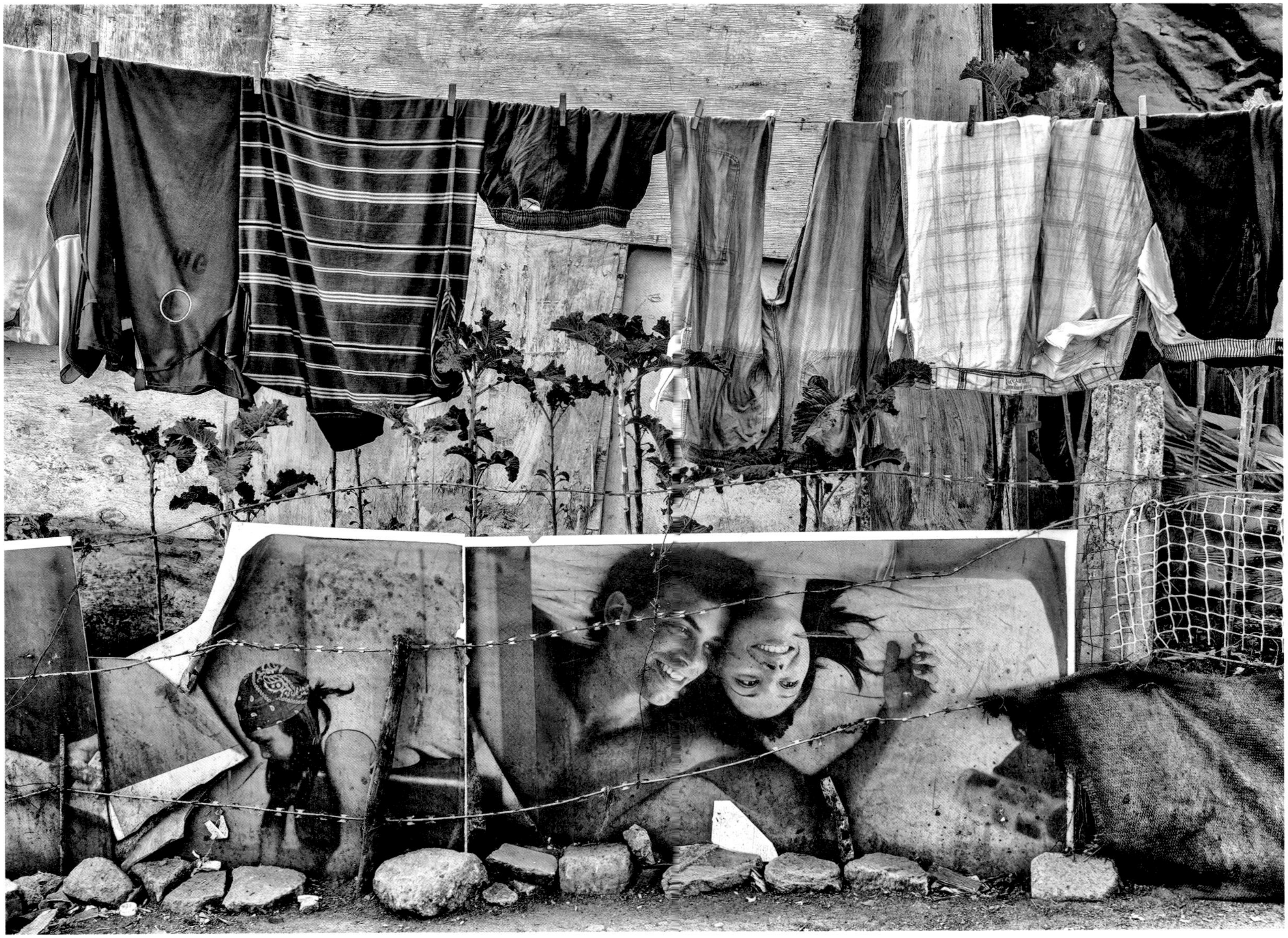

Juxtaposition #1 (September 2017)

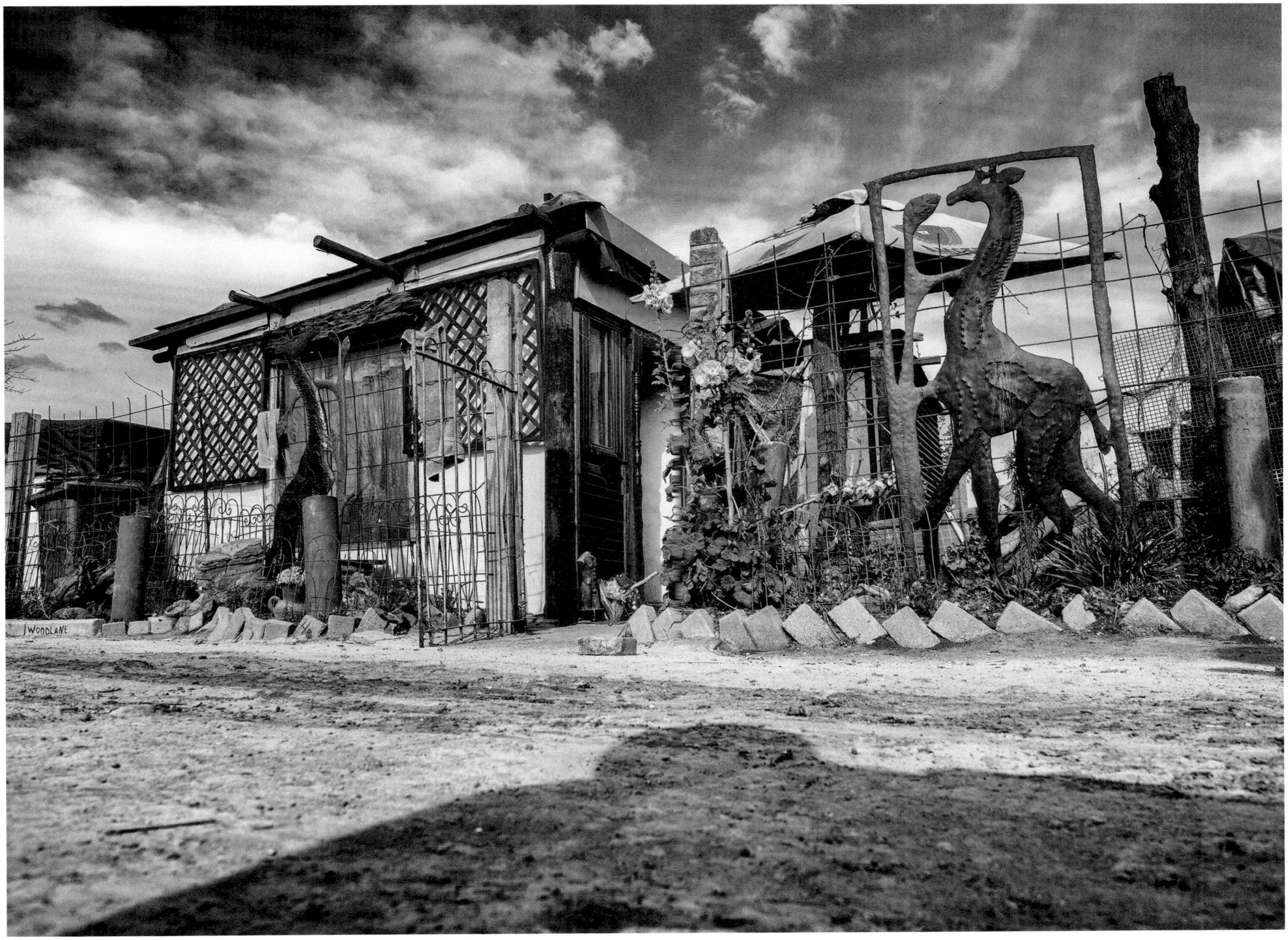

Trappings of home #1 (August 2015)

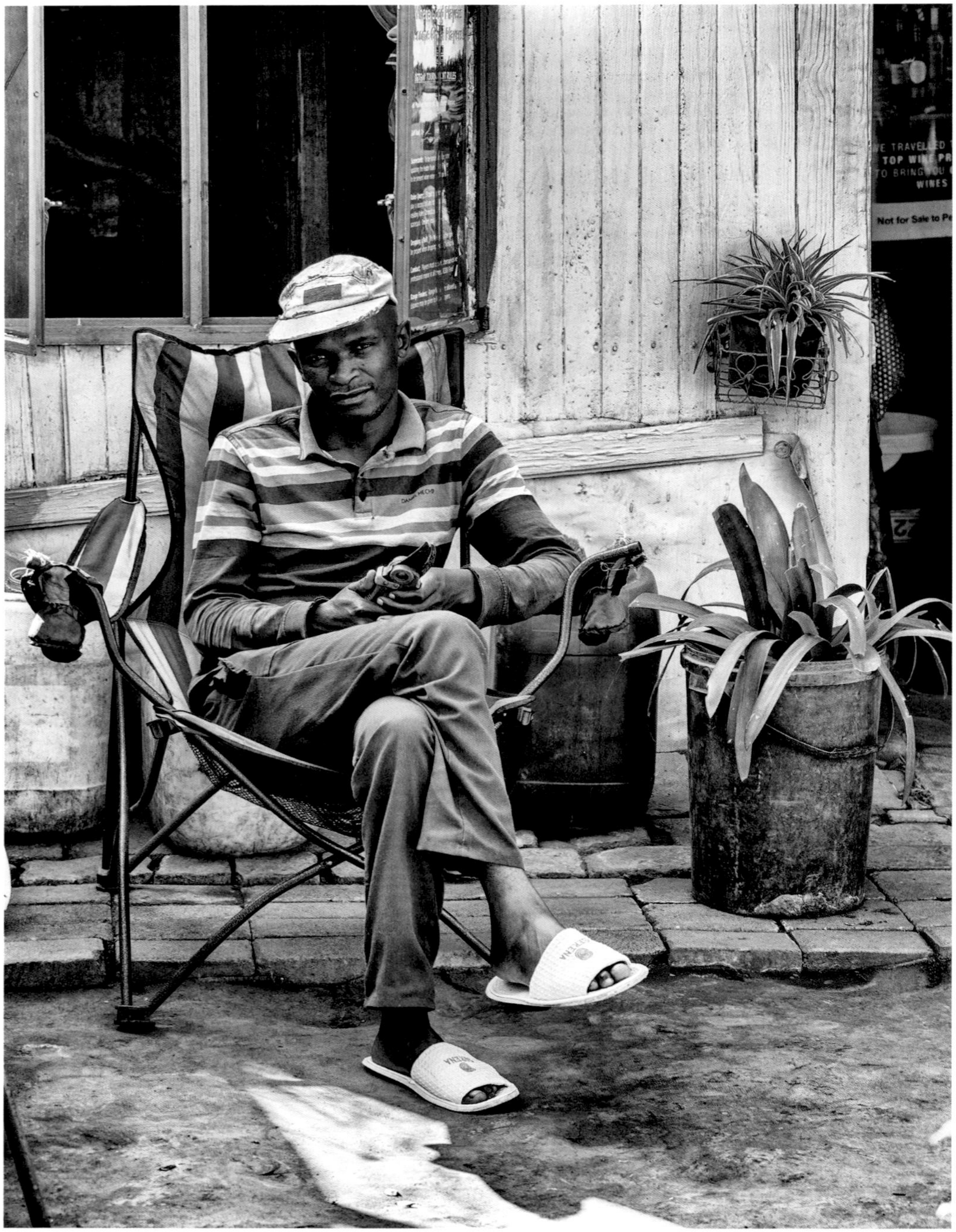

Donald's neighbor
with garden scissors
(September 2017)

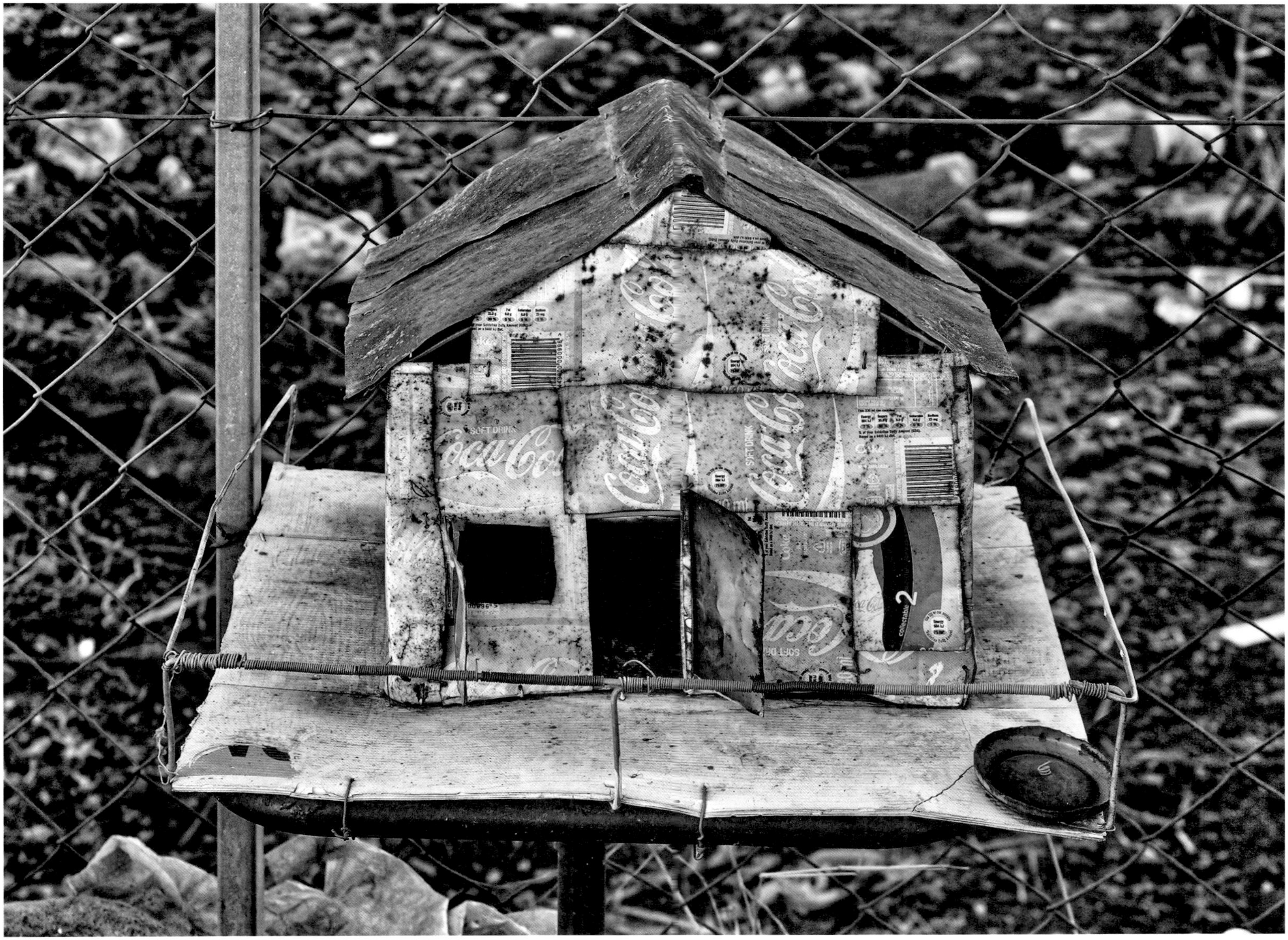

Birdhouse and lawn ornament (August 2014)

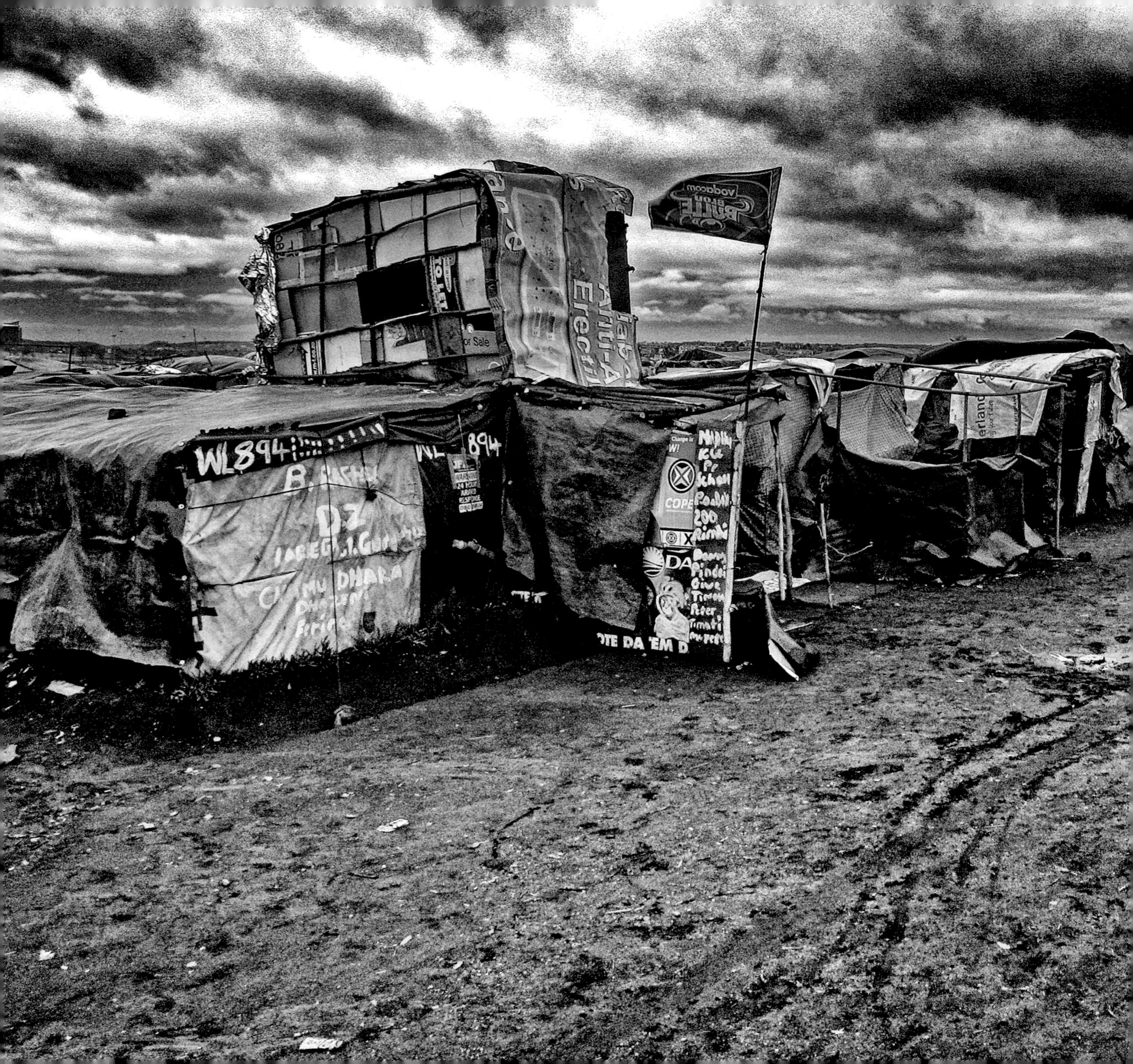
WL894
894
COPE
DA
200

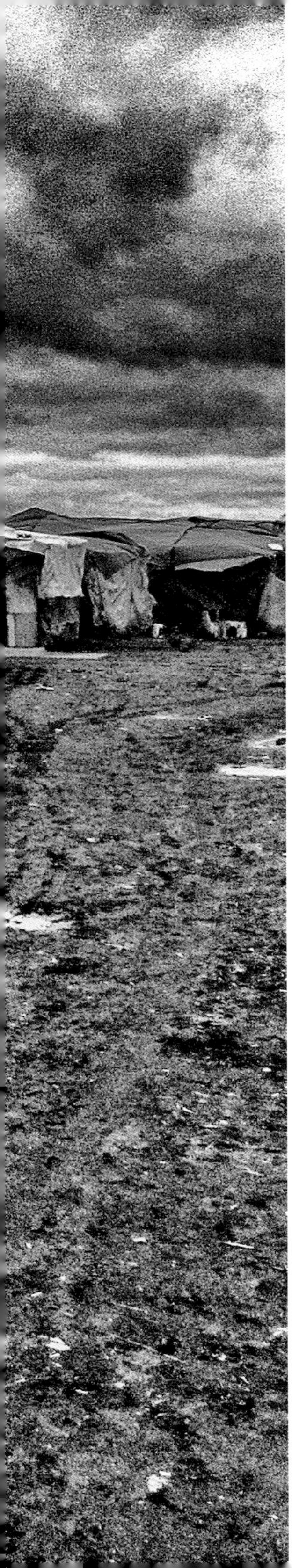

My first visit to Woodlane Village on a windy August day in 2011

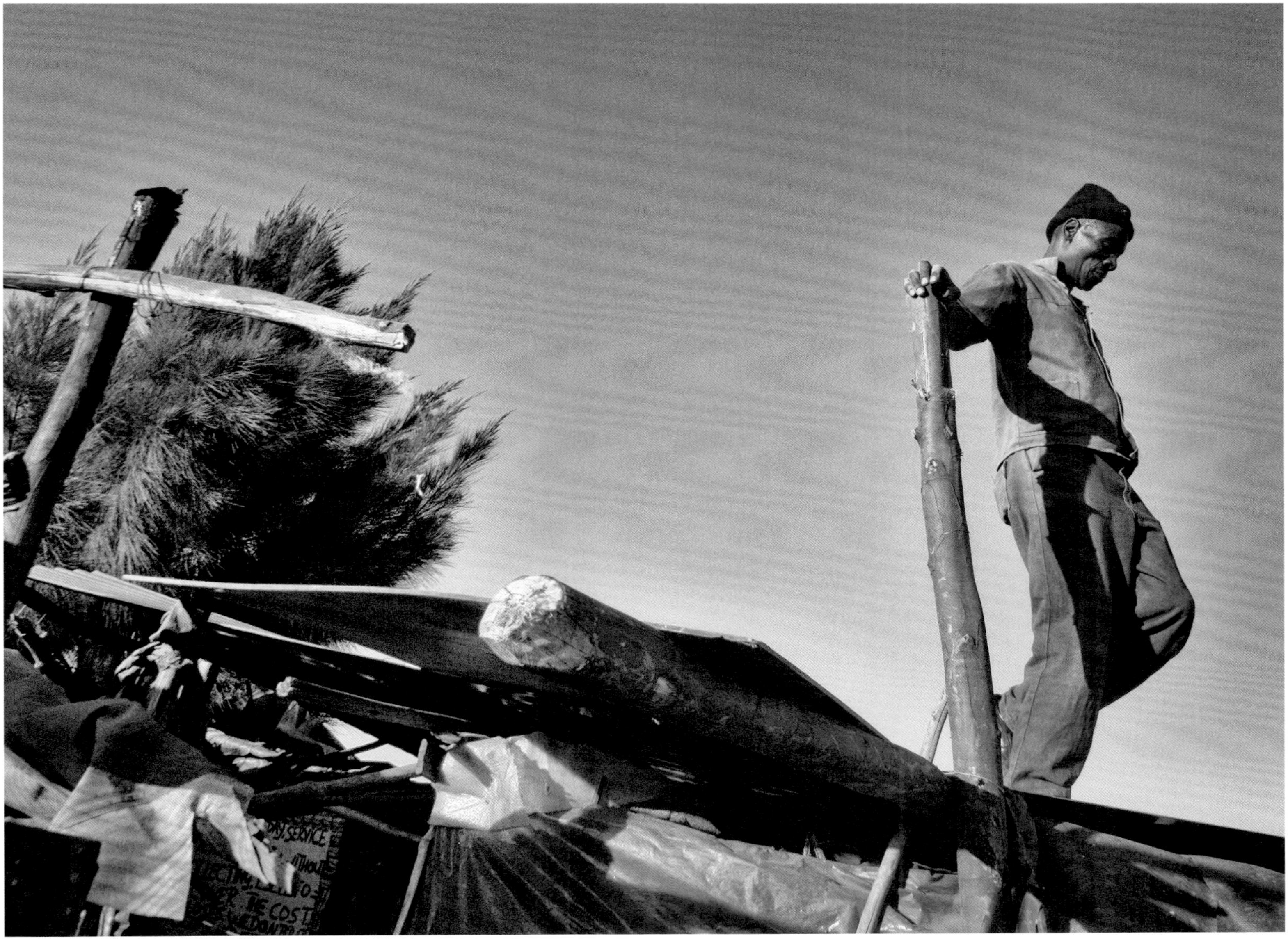

Donald repairs the roof of his shack after a fire destroyed part of his shelter (August 2013)

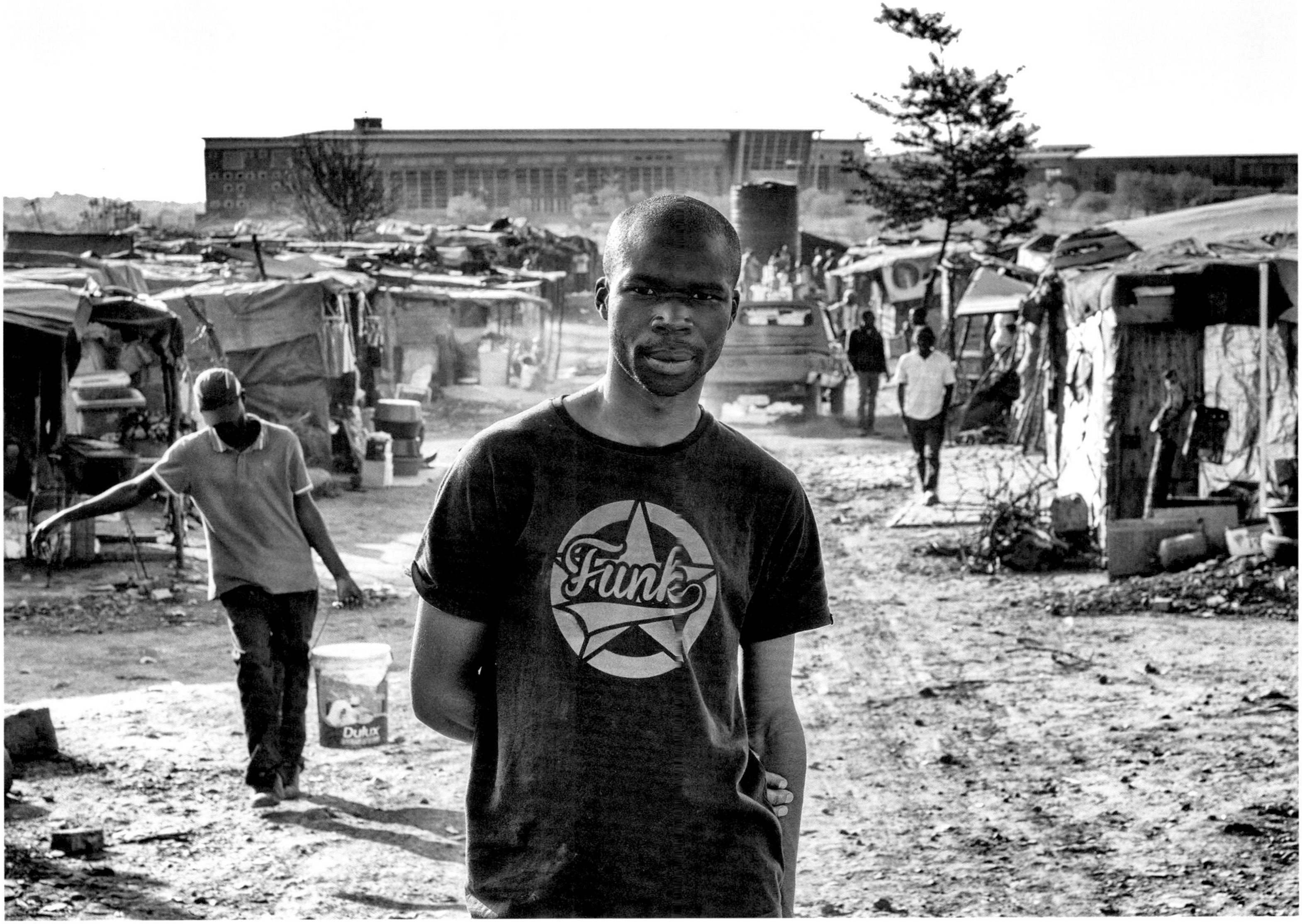

Juxtaposition #2 — NG Moreleta Church can be seen in the background. It has a congregation of over 7,000 people (August 2015)

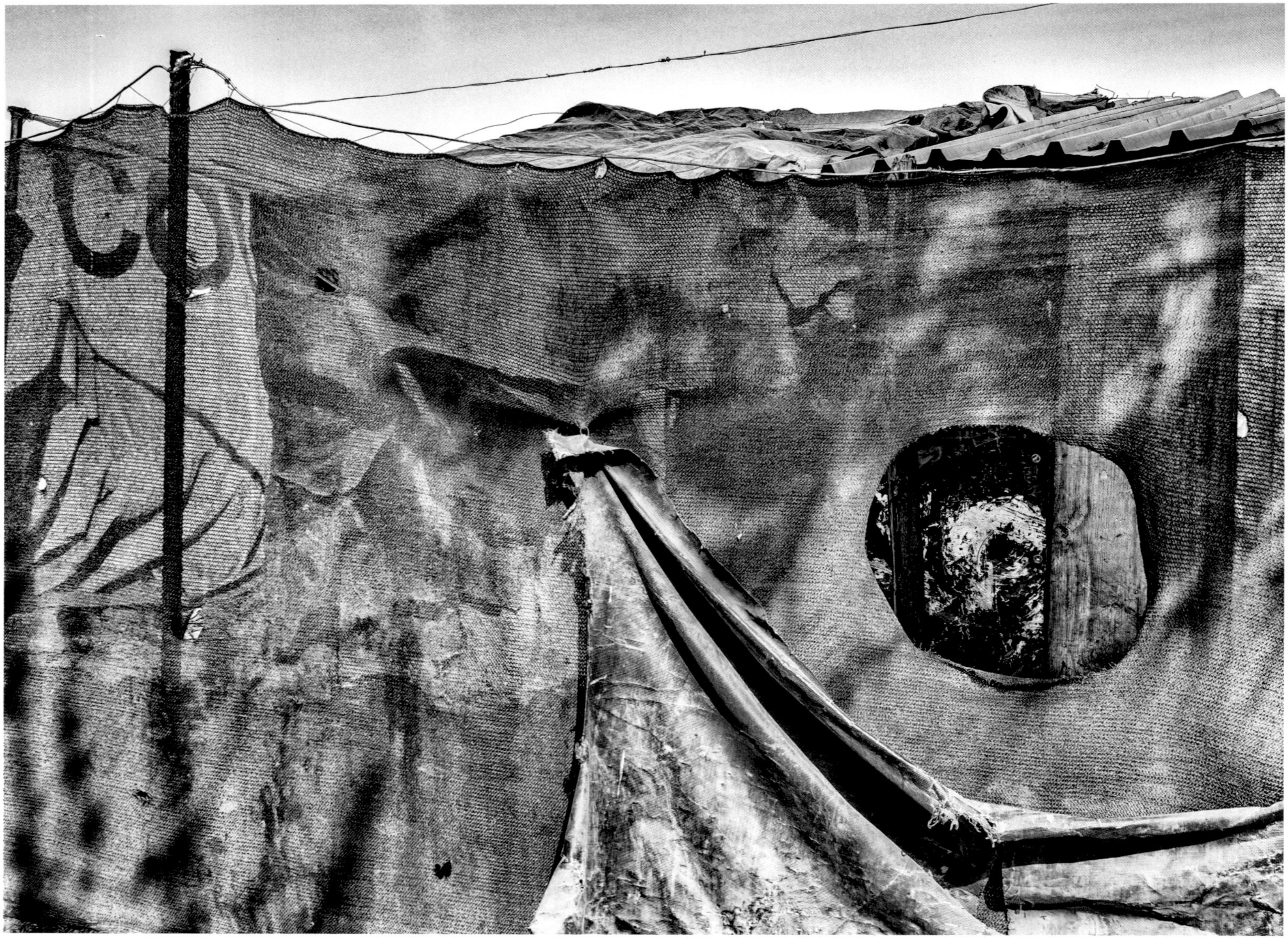

Canvas windbreak (September 2017)

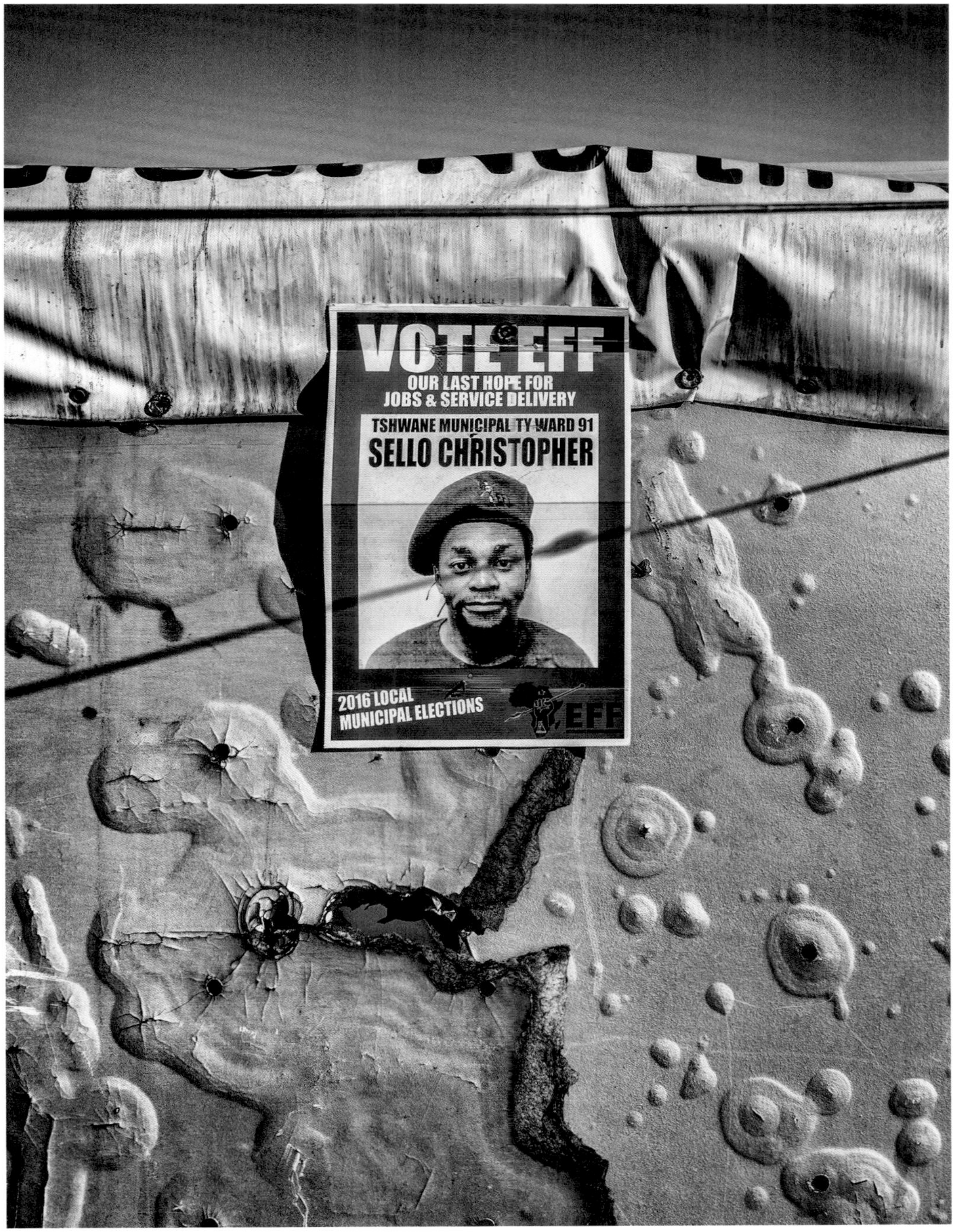

Poster for the 2016 Tshwane municipal elections (August 2016)

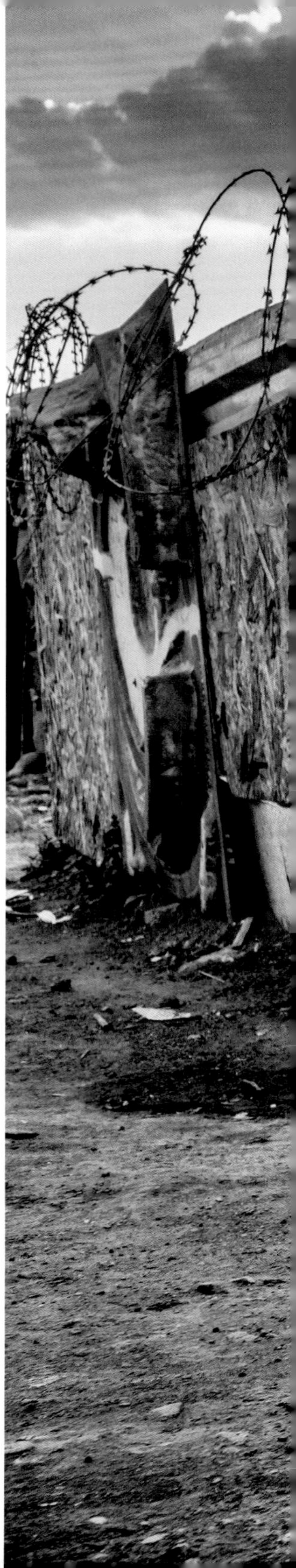

Legacy of apartheid
(August 2017)

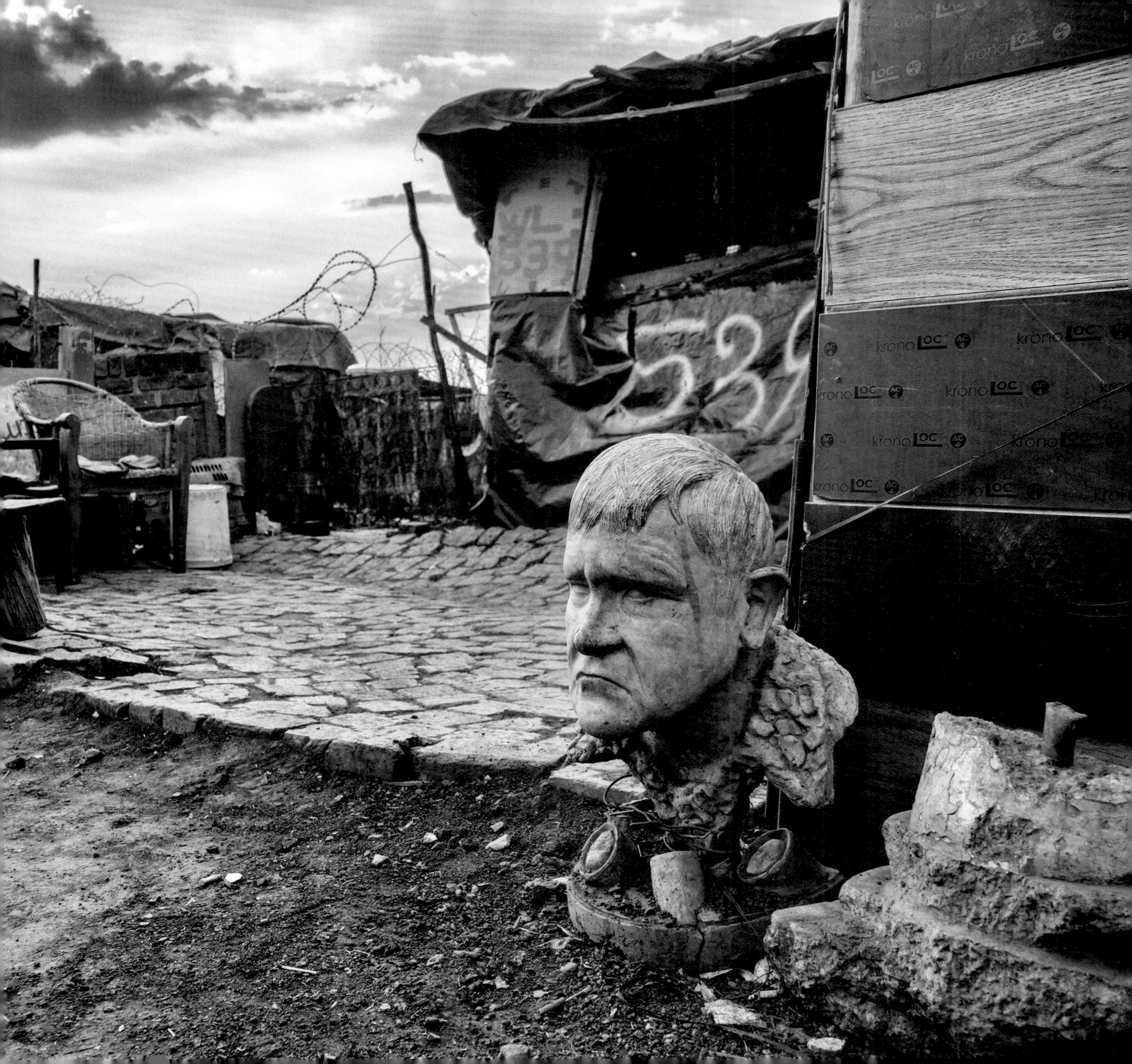
krono LOC
539

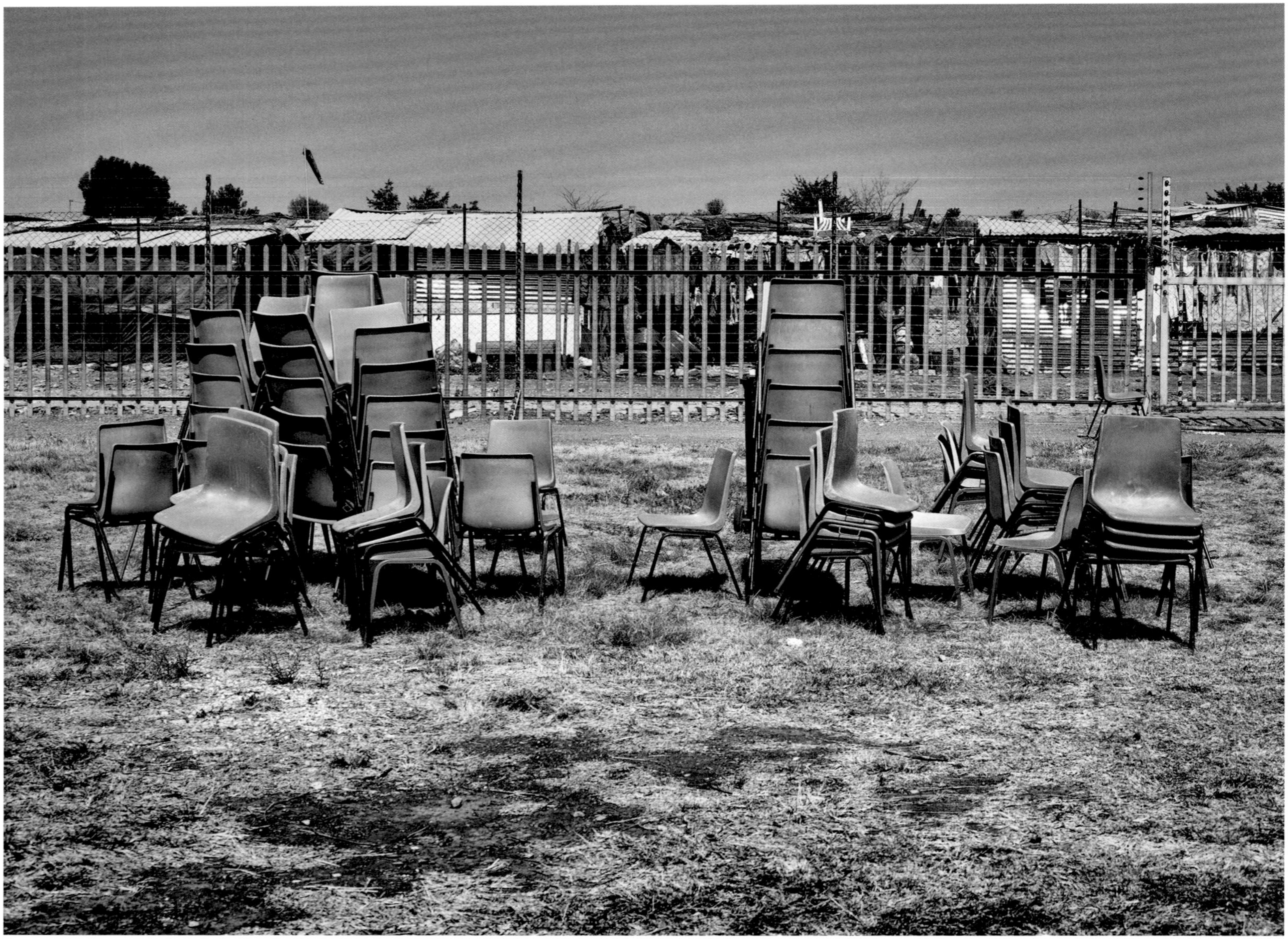

Land of enclaves and partitions—the view of the Village from NG Moreleta Church property (September 2017)

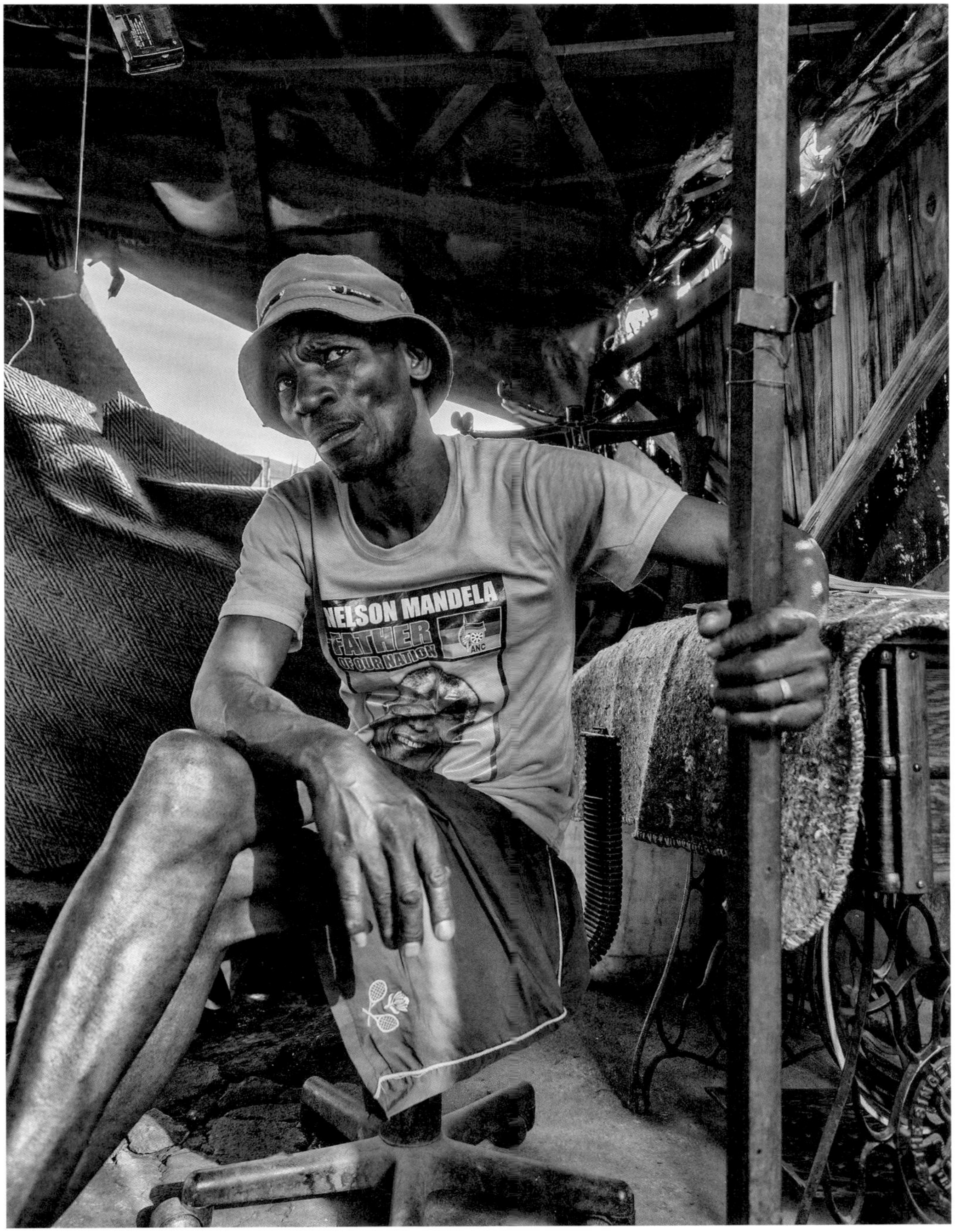

Donald with Nelson Mandela T-shirt (August 2016)

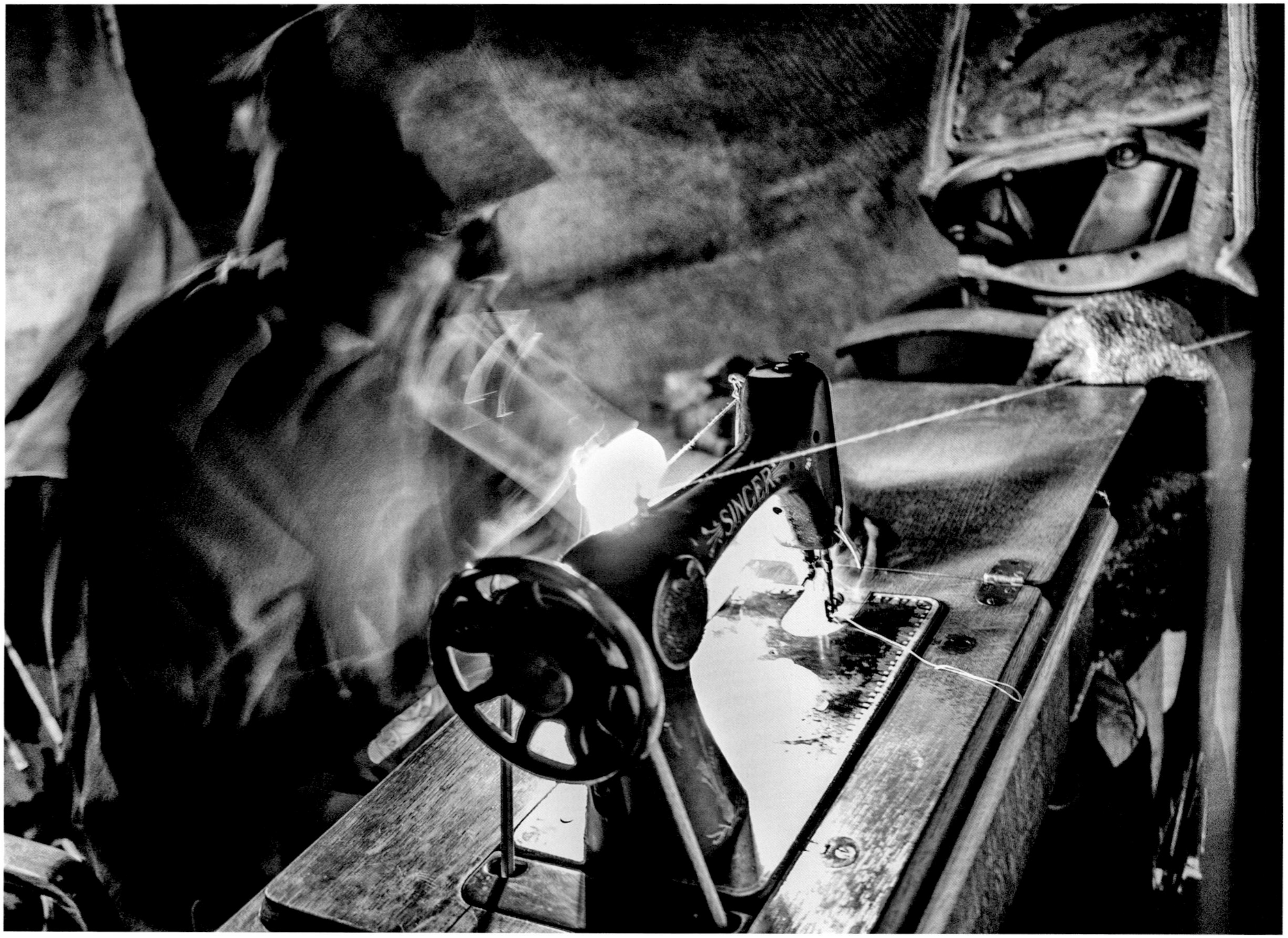

Night sewing (August 2016)

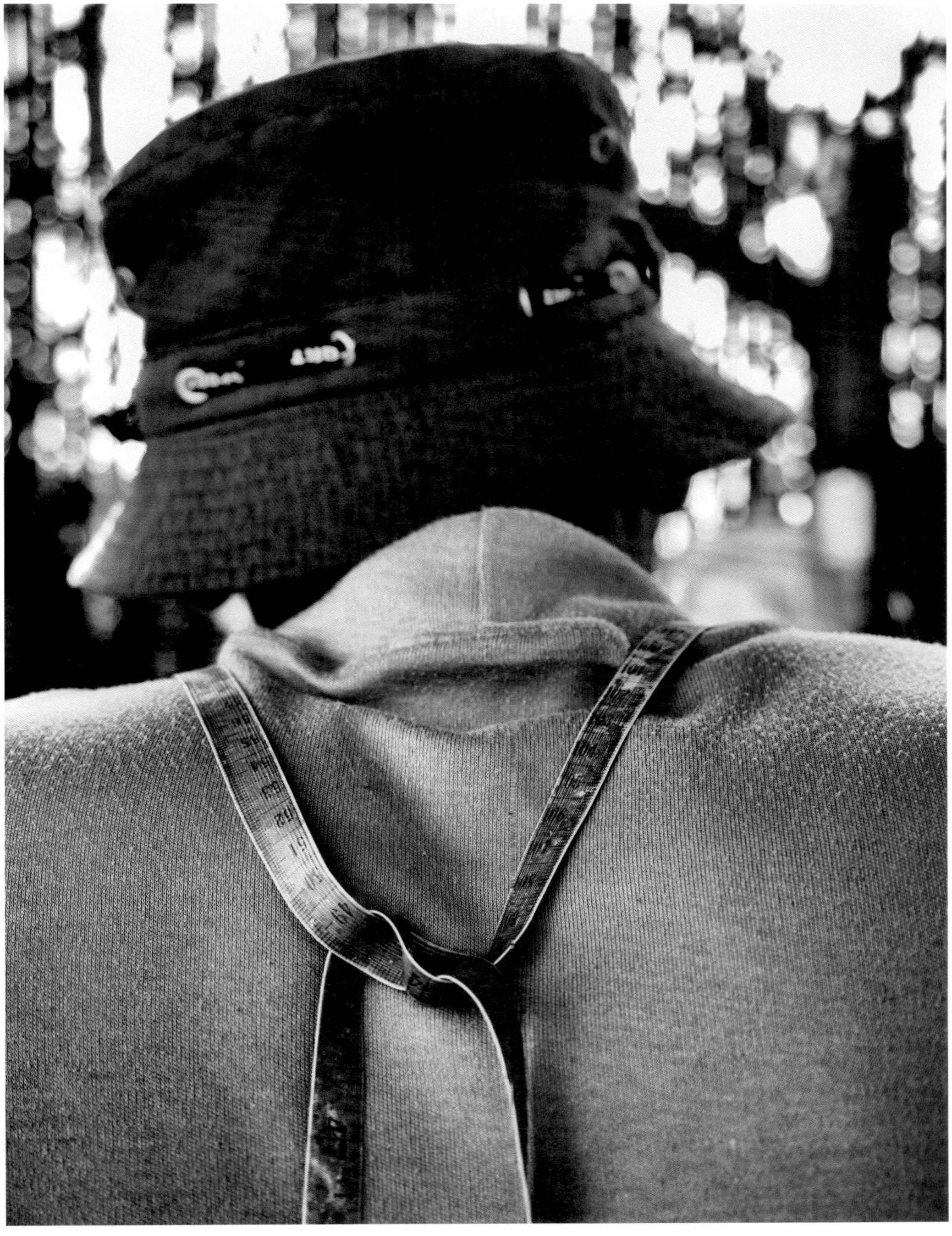

Donald, tailor and community leader (August 2015)

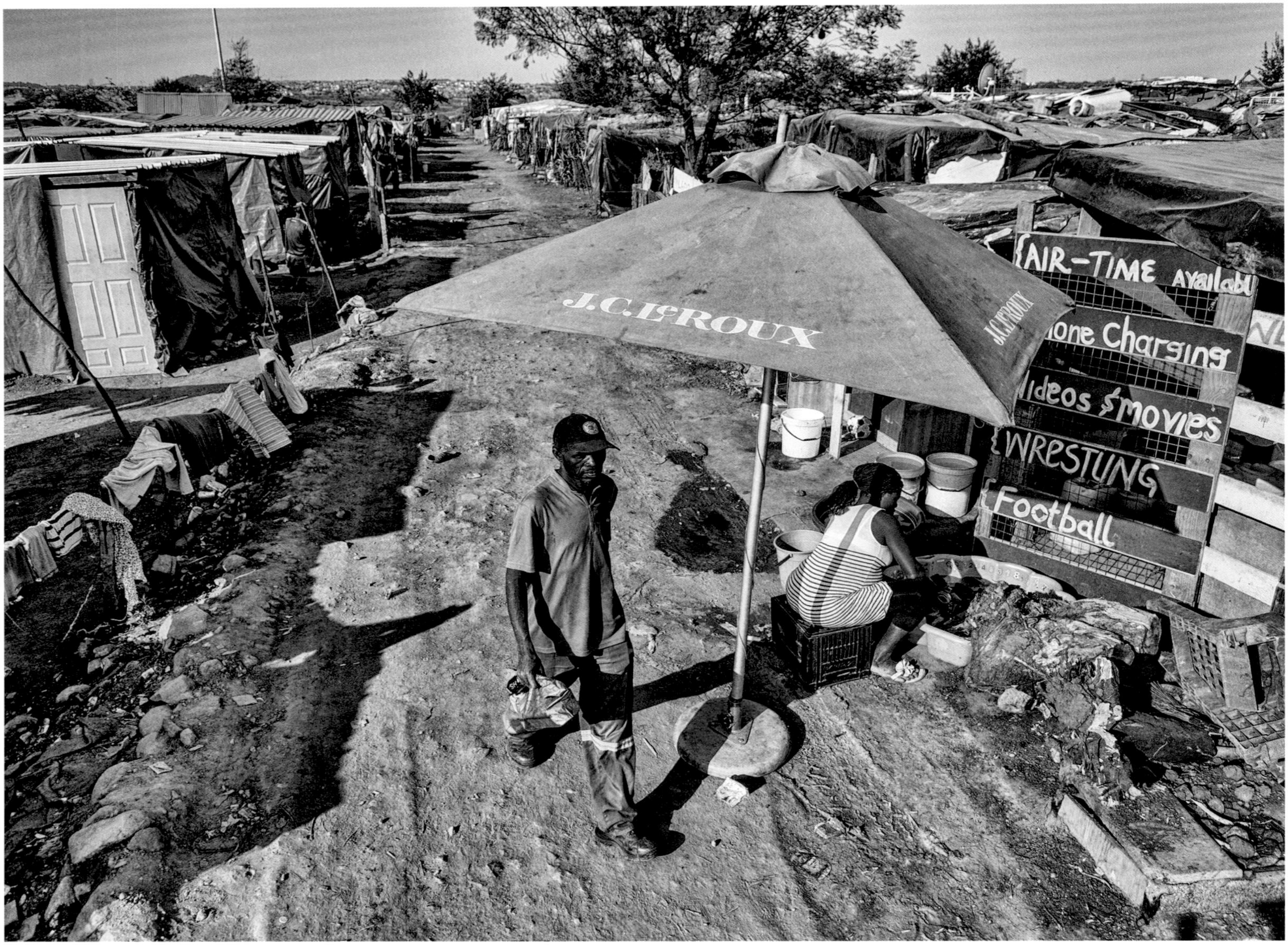

Woodlane Village, Moreleta Park, Pretoria (September 2016)

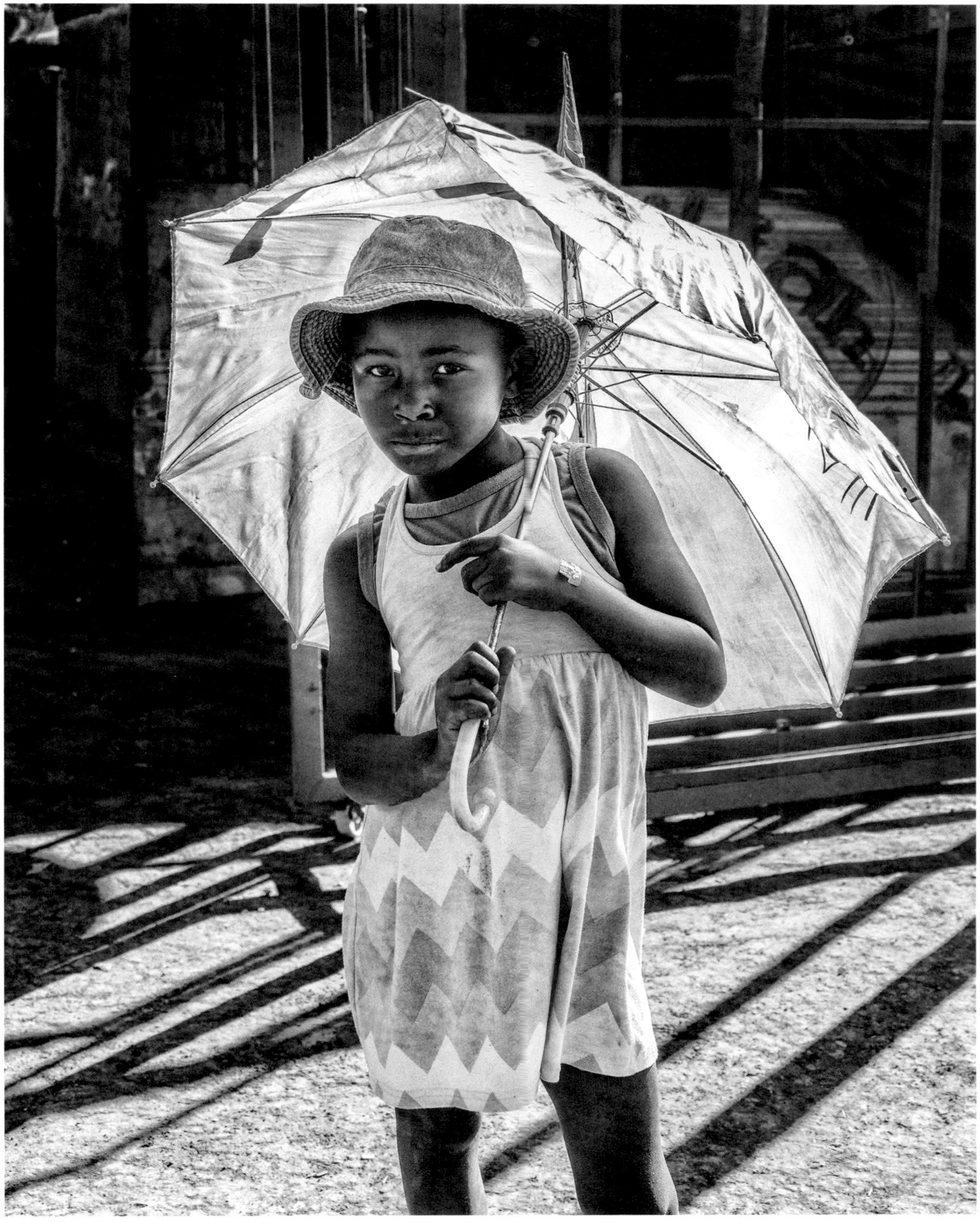

Girl with parasol
(September 2017)

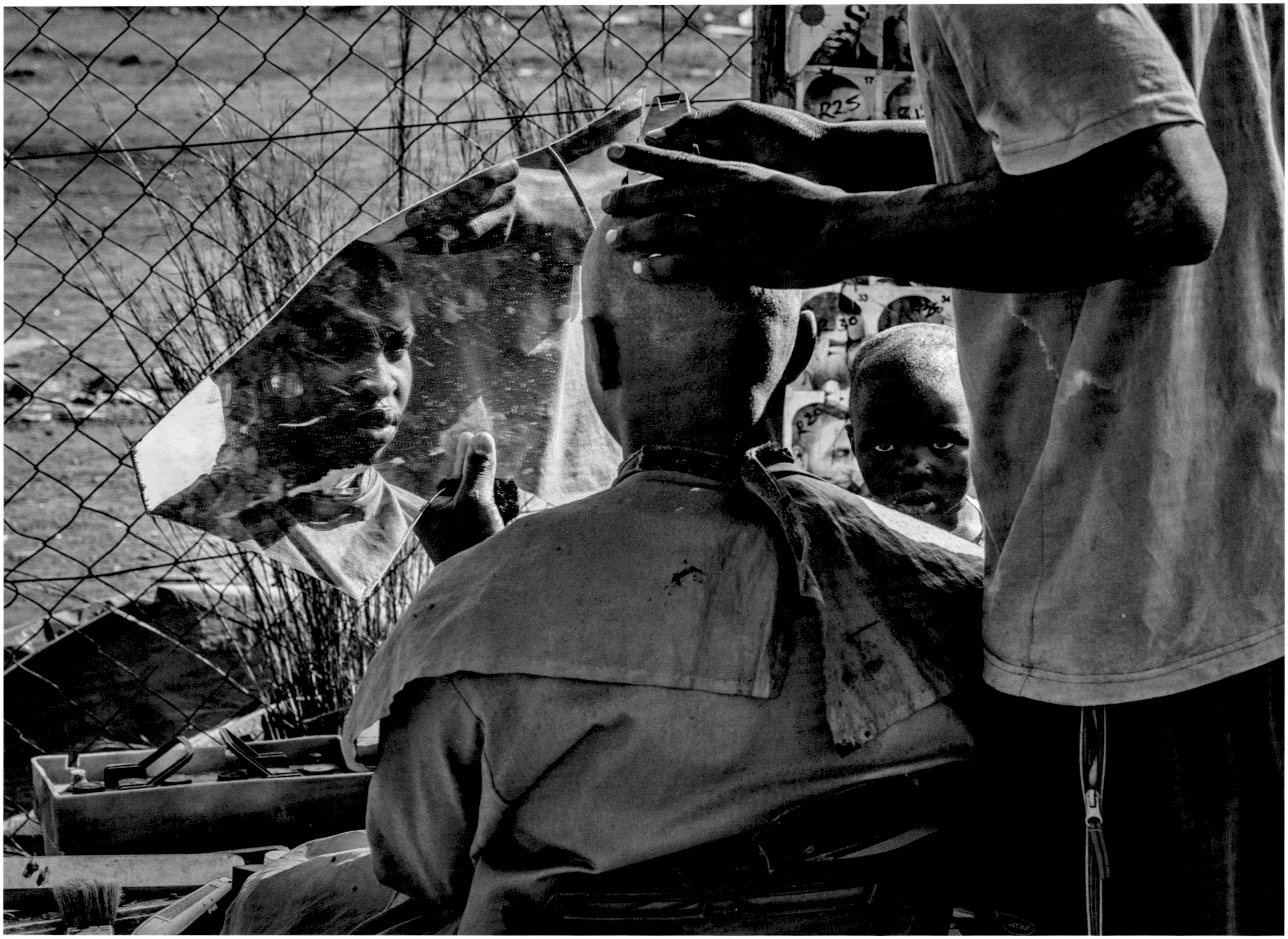

Barbershop (September 2017)

Style guide and price list (September 2017)

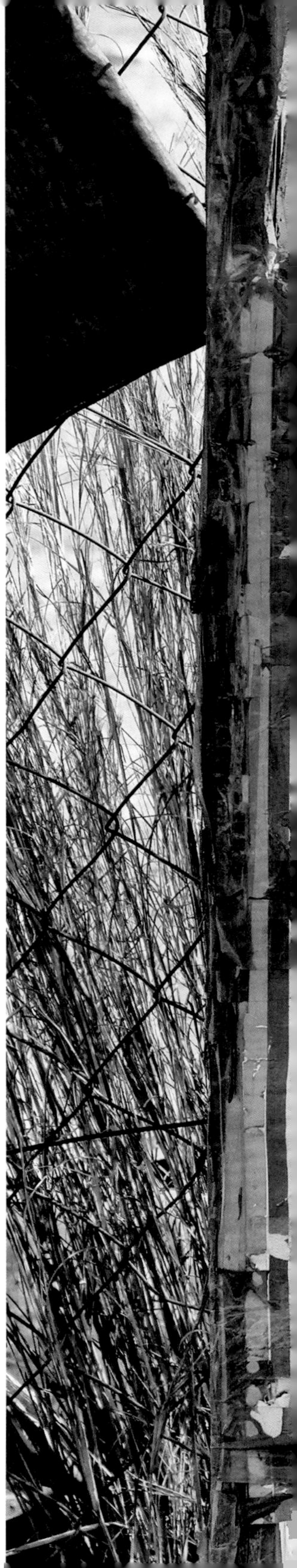

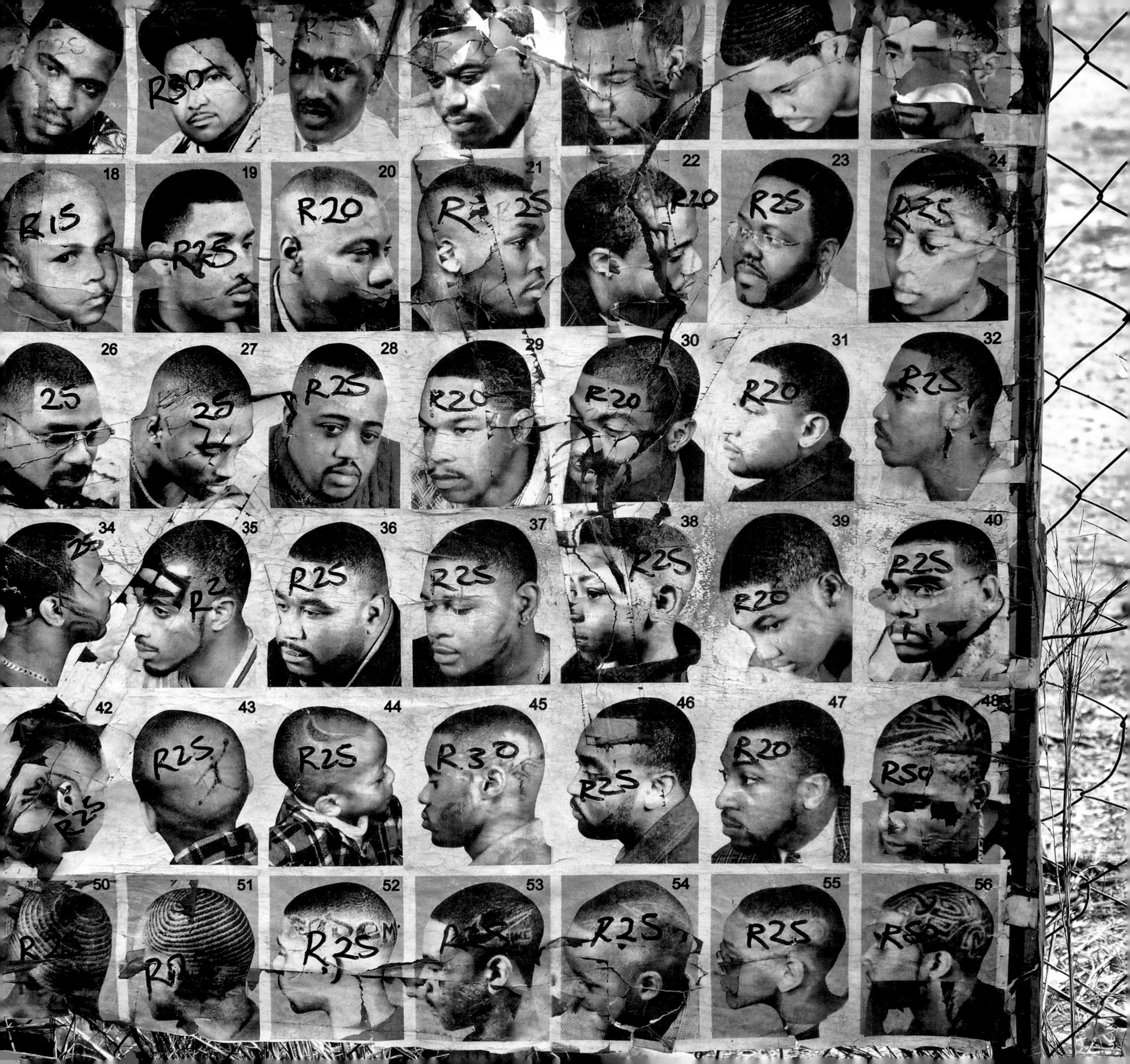
R30
18
R15
19
R25
20
R20
22
R20
23
R25
24
R25
26
25
27
25
28
R25
29
R20
30
R20
31
R20
32
R25
34
25
35
R20
36
R25
37
R25
38
R25
39
R20
40
R25
42
R25
43
R25
44
R25
45
R30
46
R25
47
R20
48
R50
50
51
52
R25
53
54
R25
55
R25
56
R50

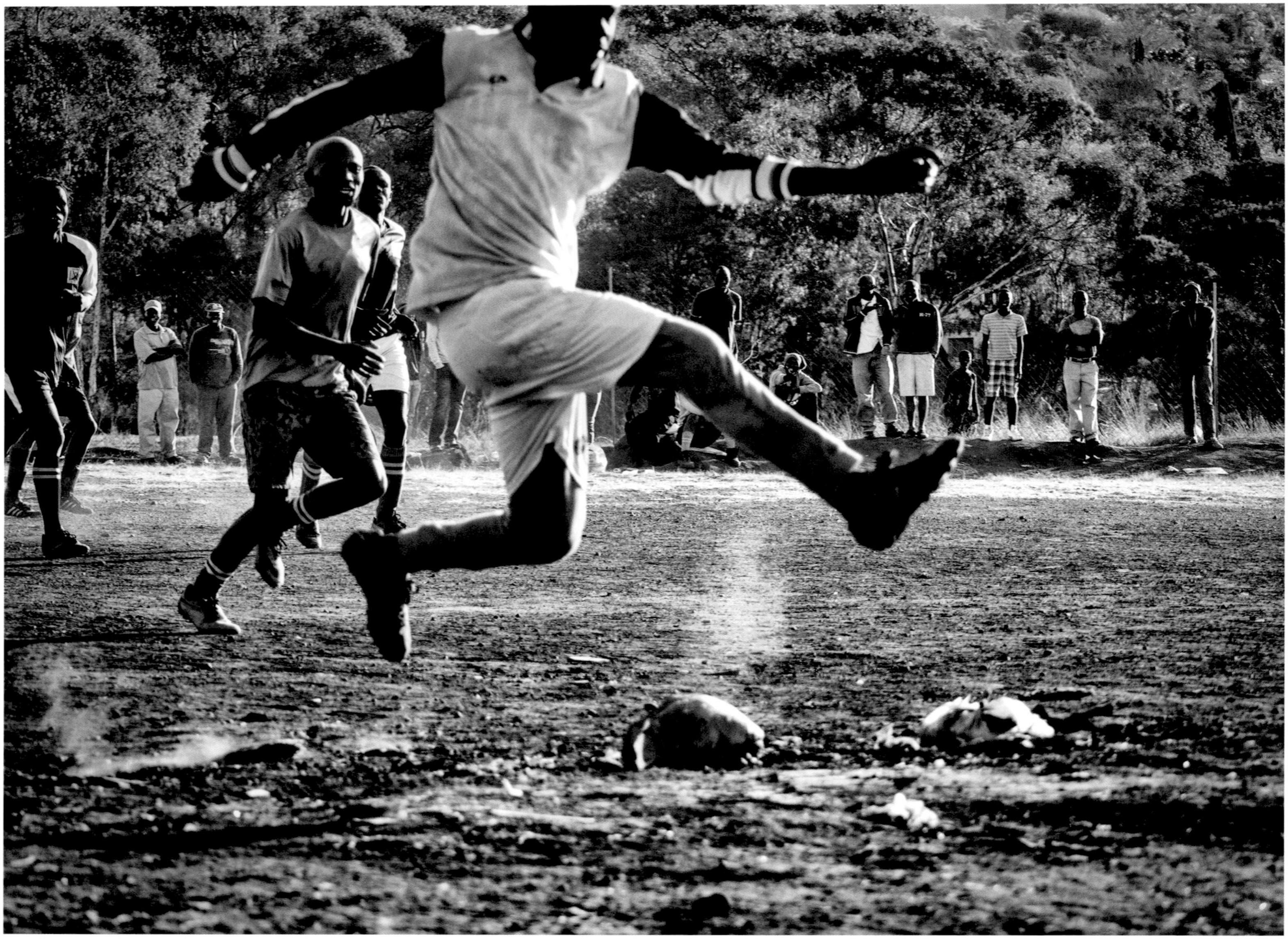

Sunday afternoon football match (August 2015)

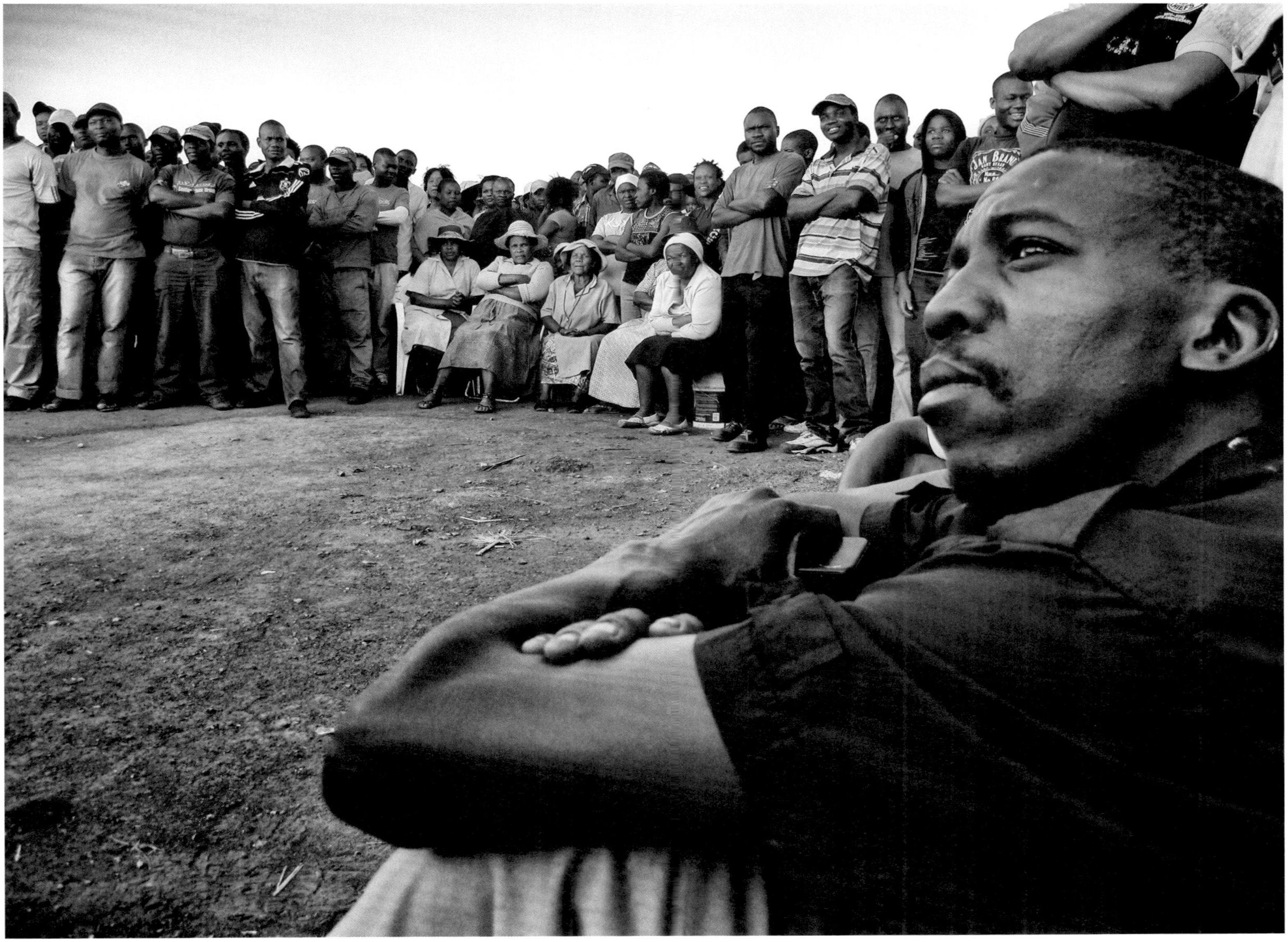

Community meeting on crime and safety (October 2012)

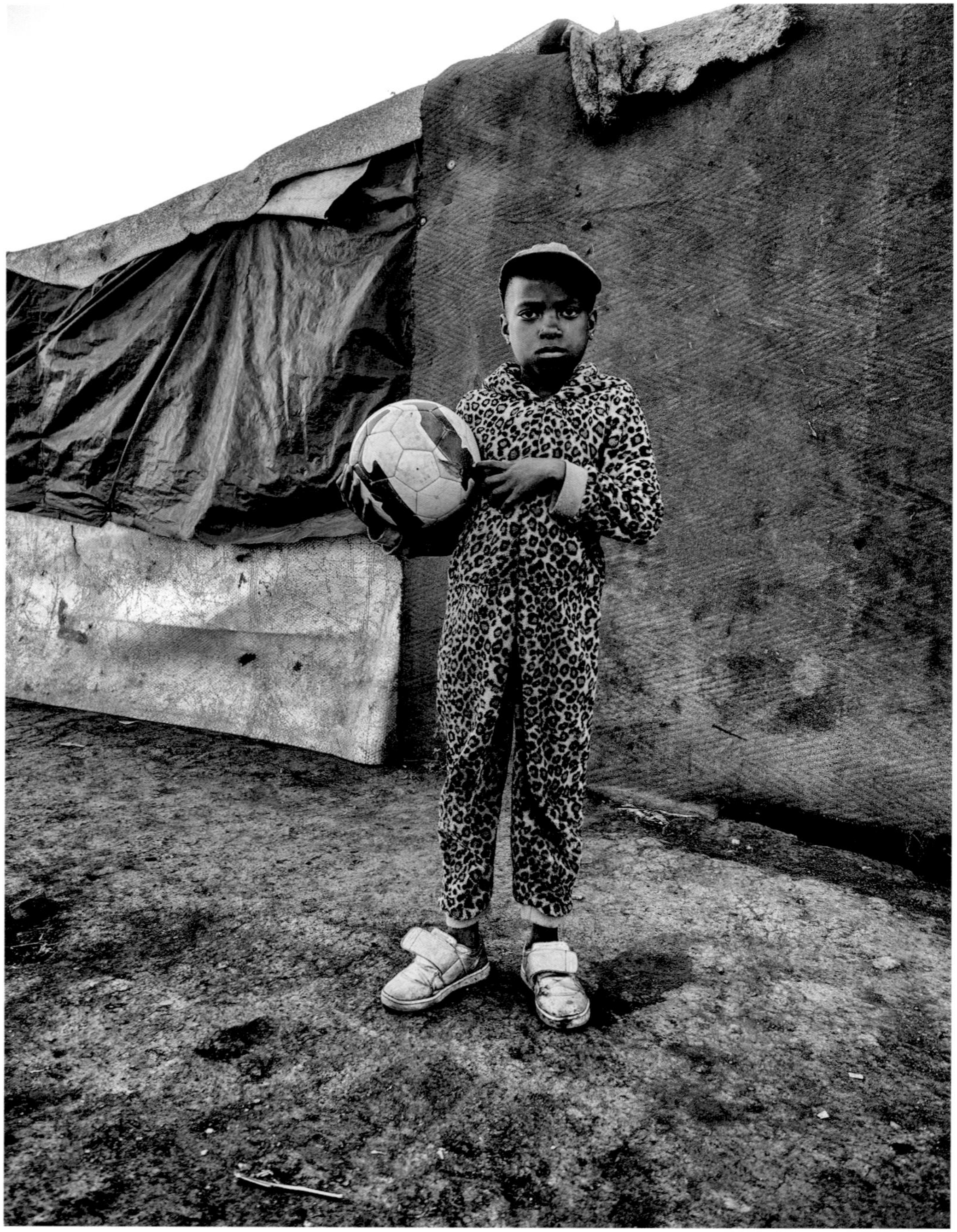

Girl in leopard
suit with football
(August 2015)

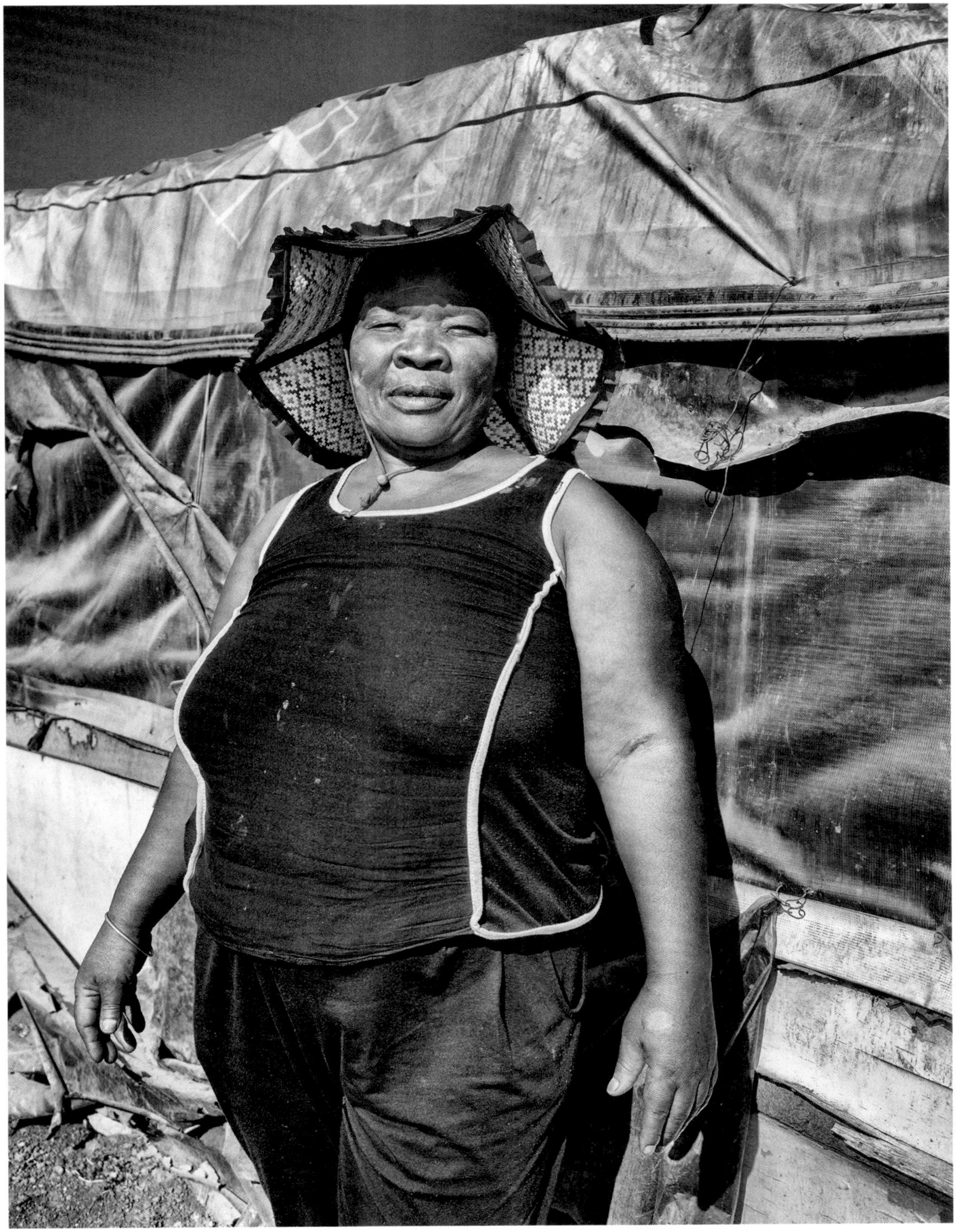

Thembi, neighbor of Donald (August 2015)

"Shack" means any temporary shelter, building, hut, tent, dwelling or similar structure which does not comply with the provisions of the National Building Regulations and Building Standards Act, 1977 (Act 103 of 1977), the regulations promulgated under that Act and the Municipality's Building Control By-laws and which is primarily used for residential purposes.

— City of Tshwane Metropolitan Municipality By-laws Relating to the Management and Control of Informal Settlements

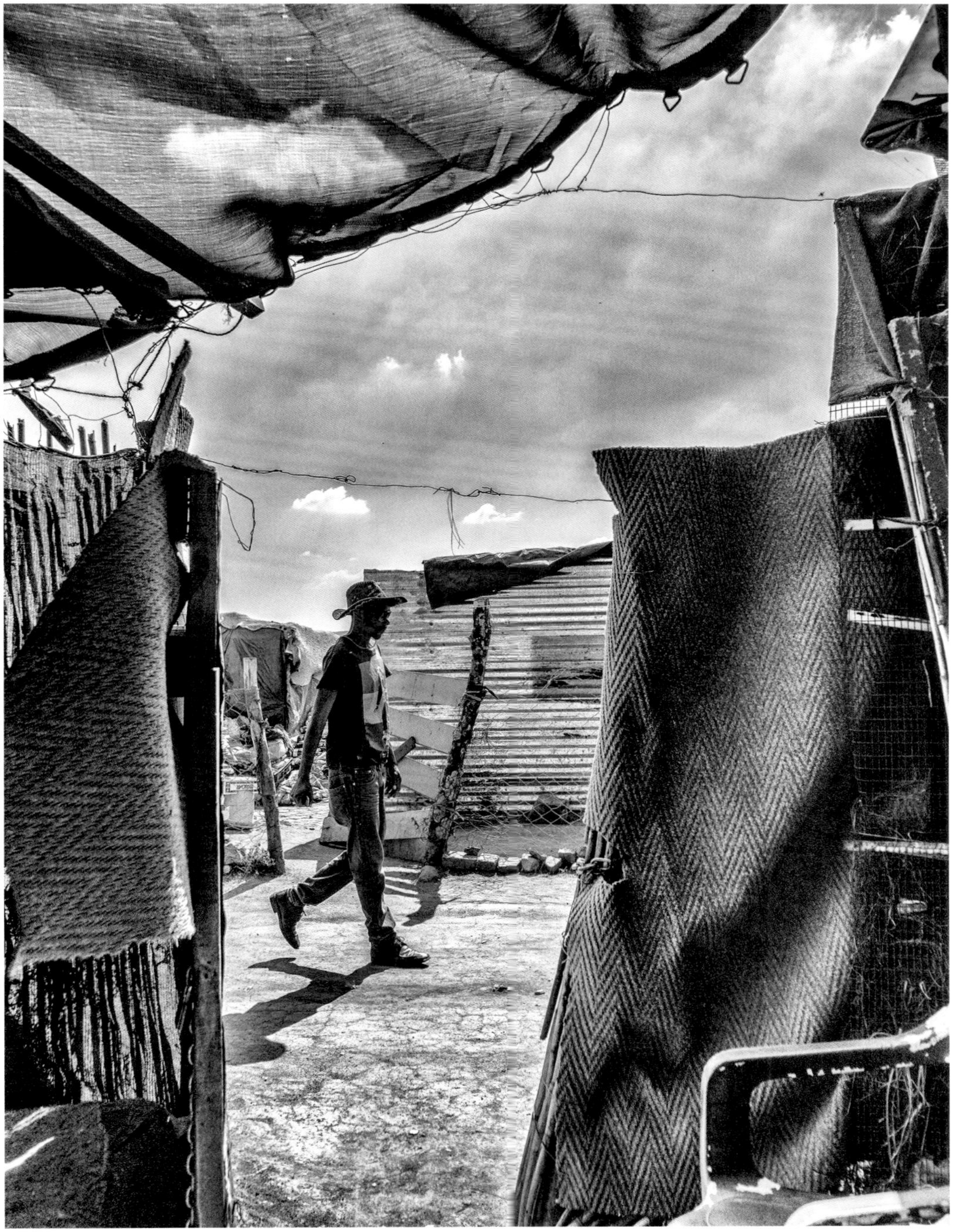

View from Donald's stand (August 2017)

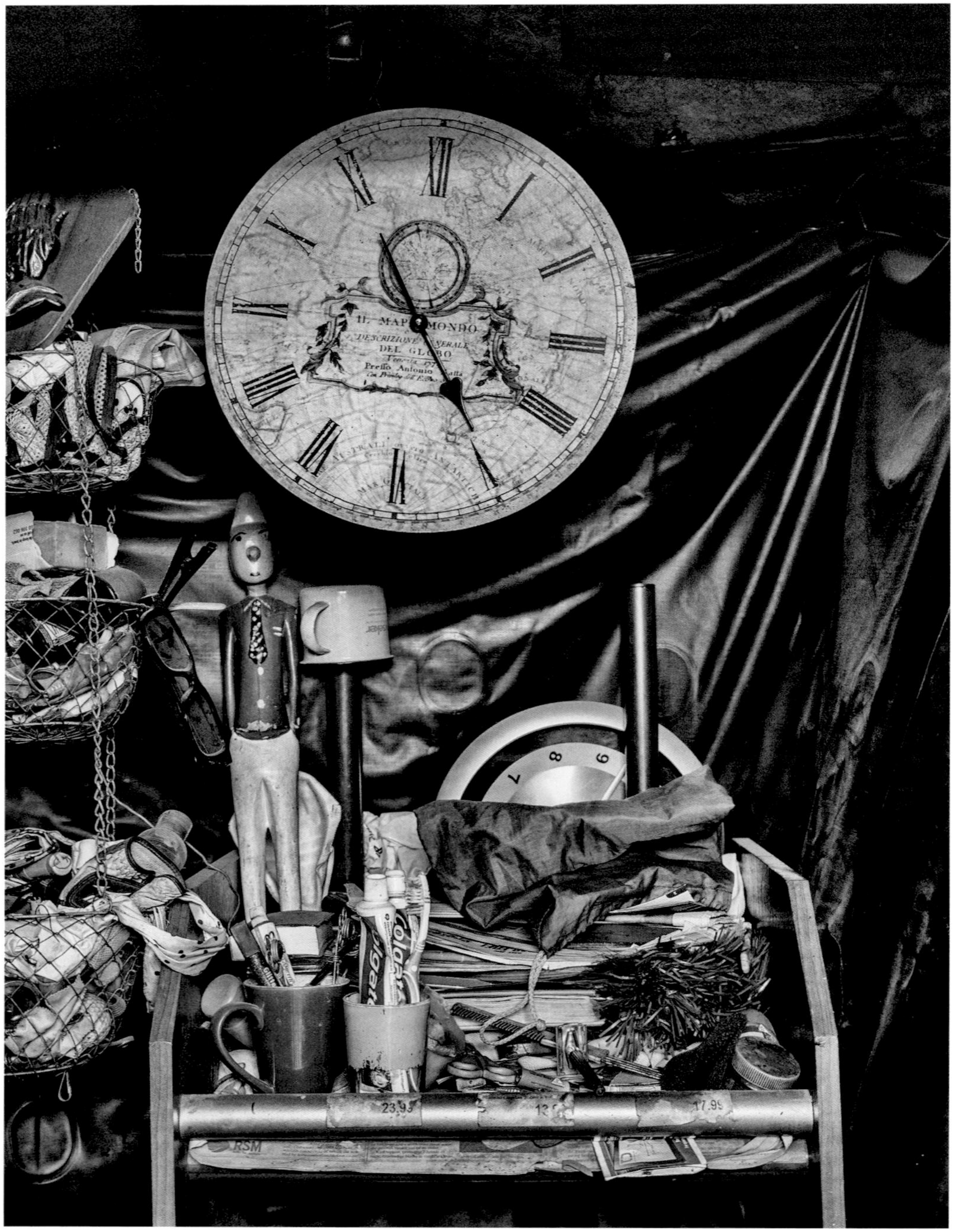

Trappings of home #2
(August 2015)

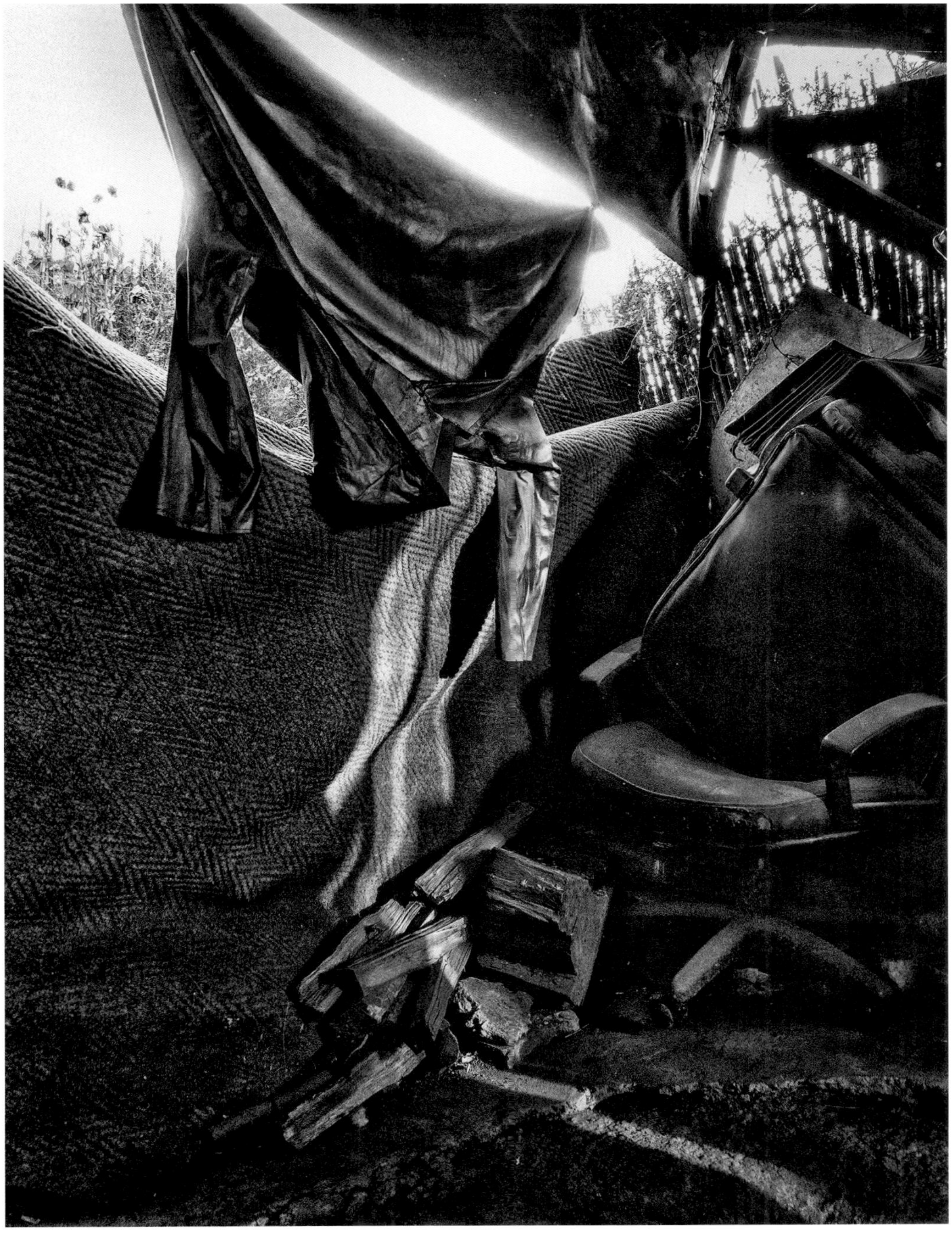

Rain jacket and firewood
(August 2017)

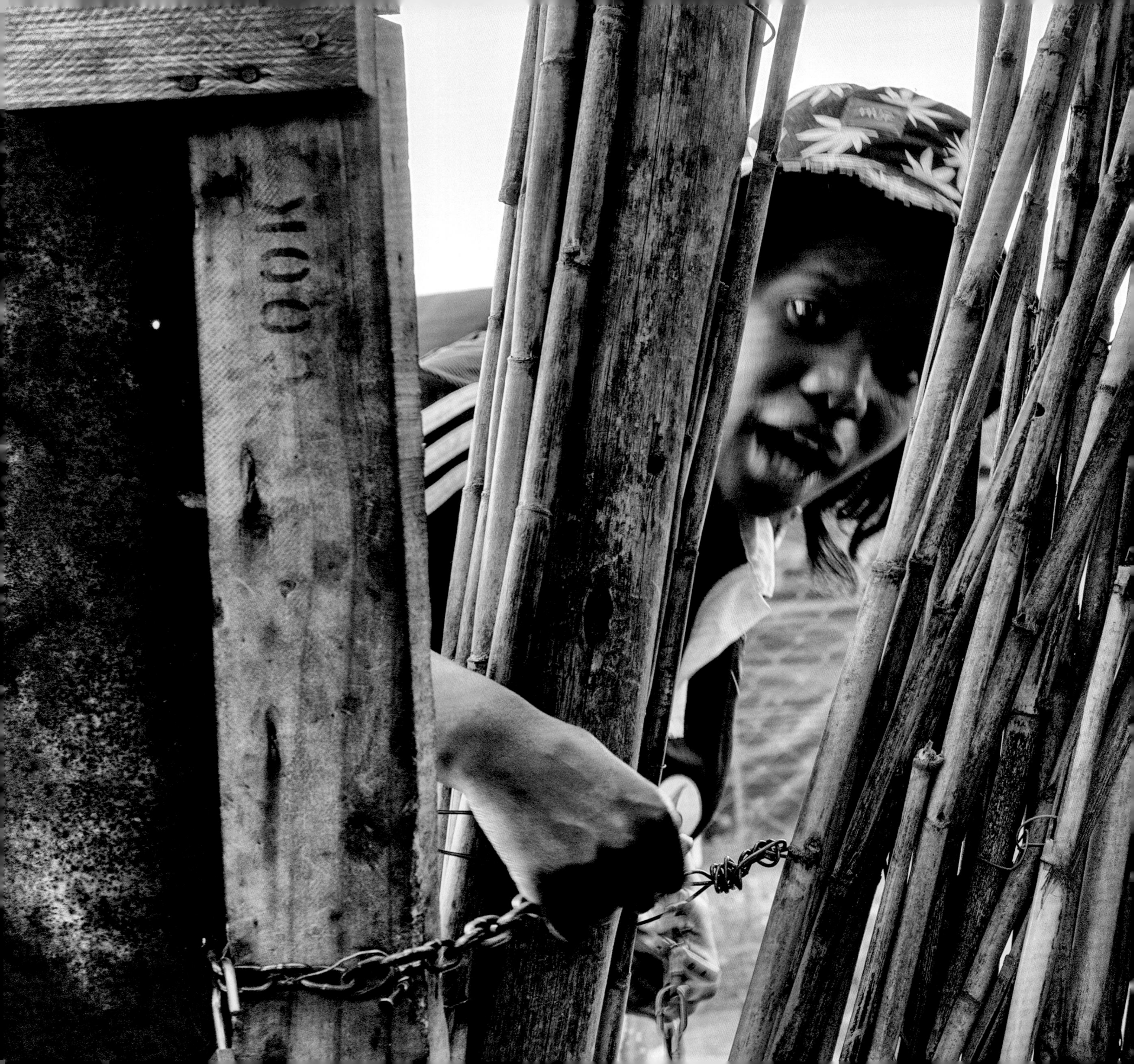

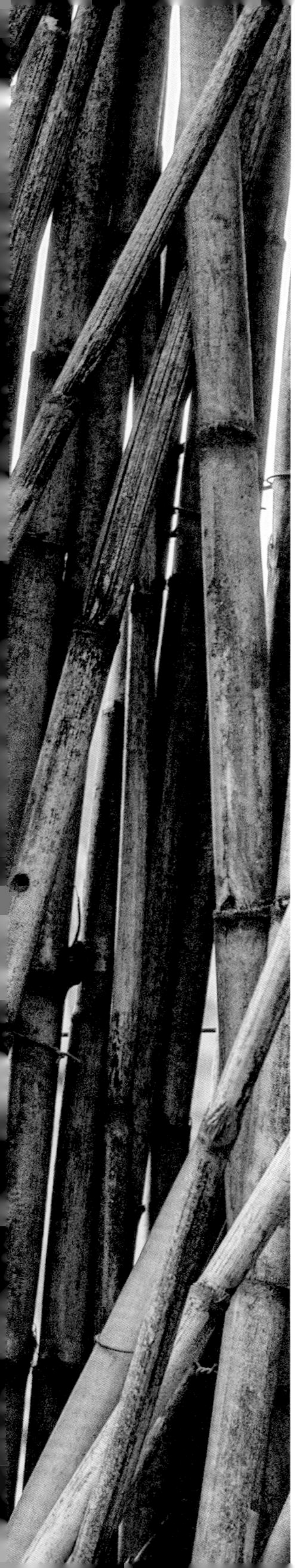

Good fences make good
neighbors (August 2015)

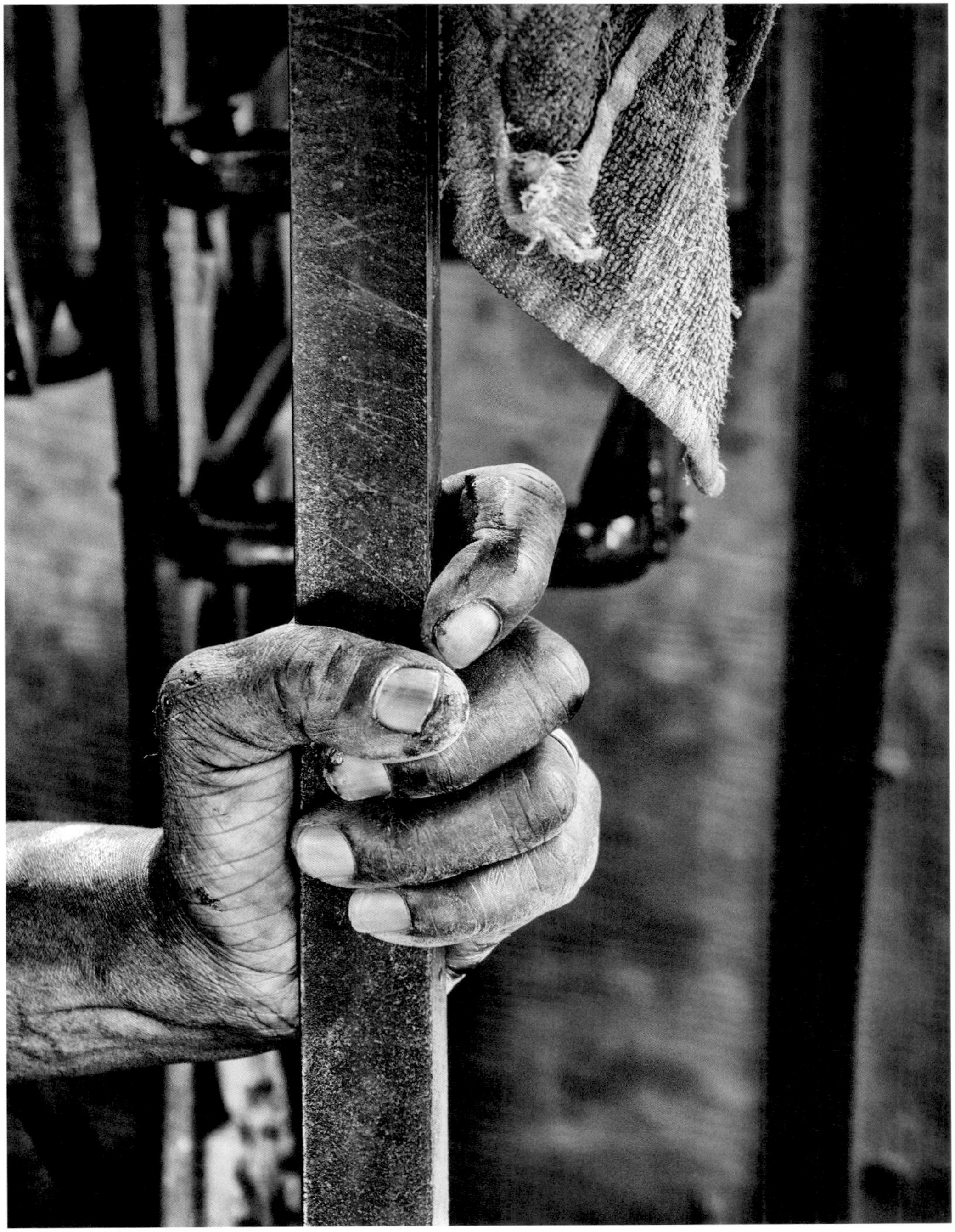

Donald's left hand
with wedding band
(August 2017)

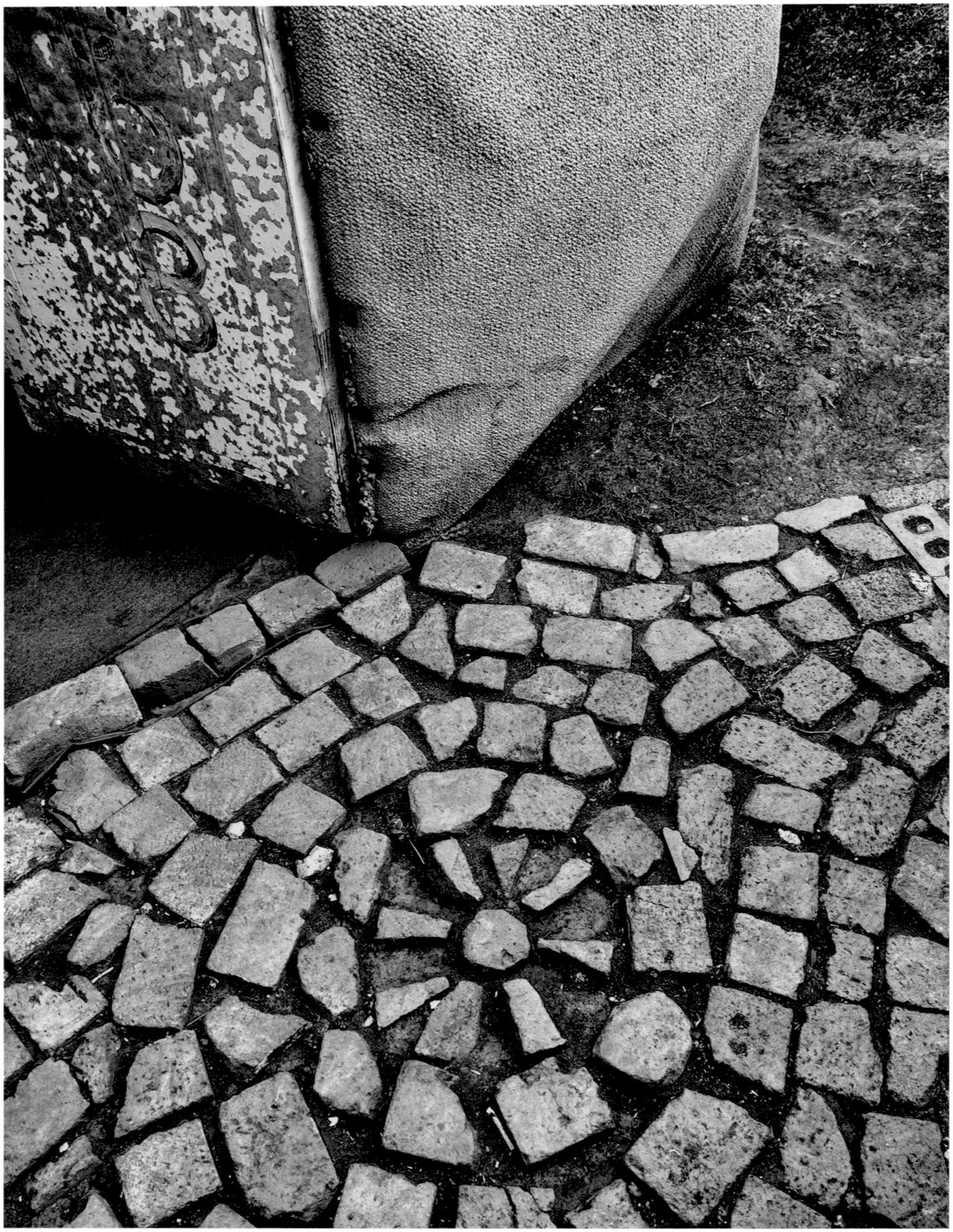

Brickwork in the courtyard of Donald (August 2015)

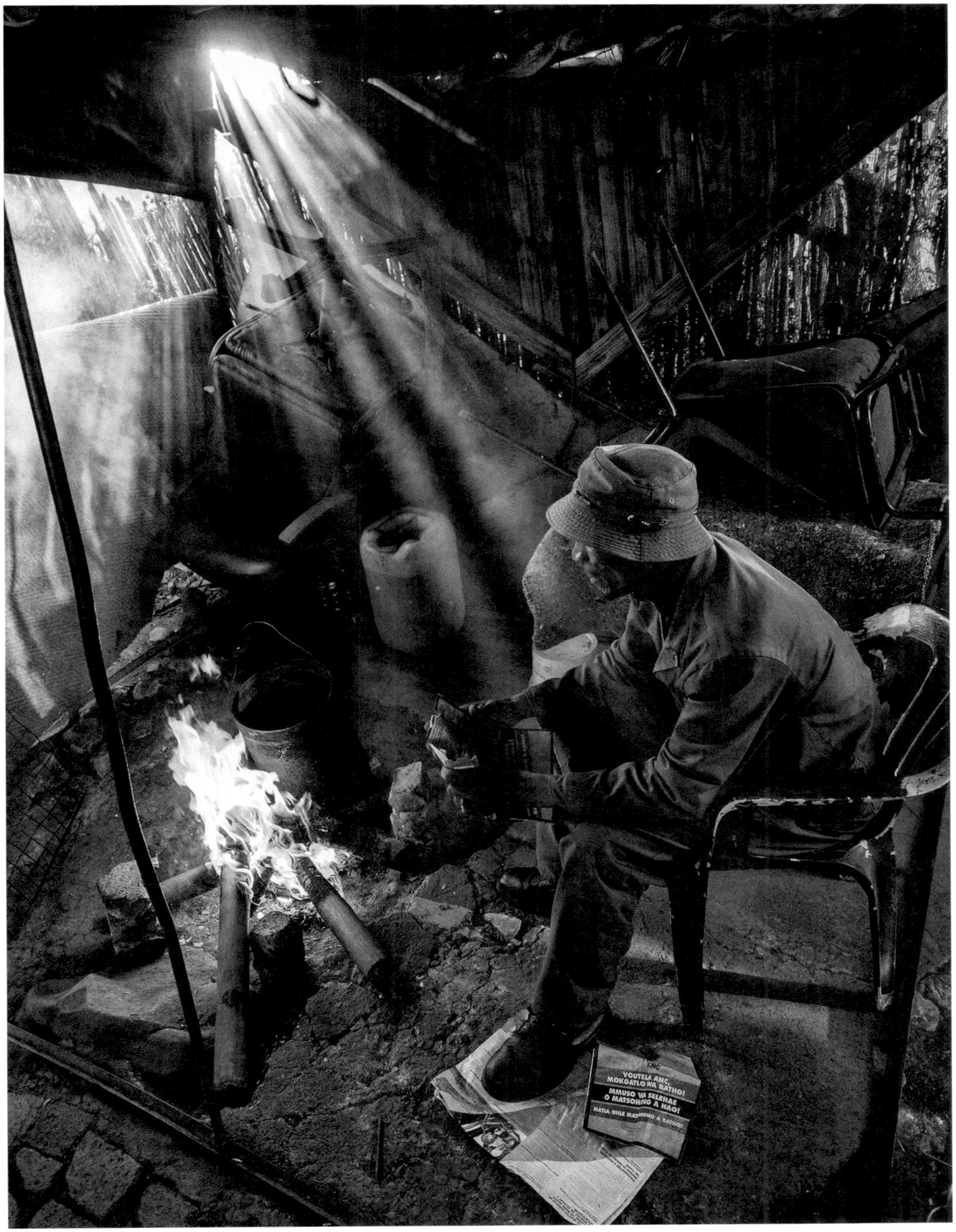

Stoking home fires with
the ANC manifesto
(August 2016)

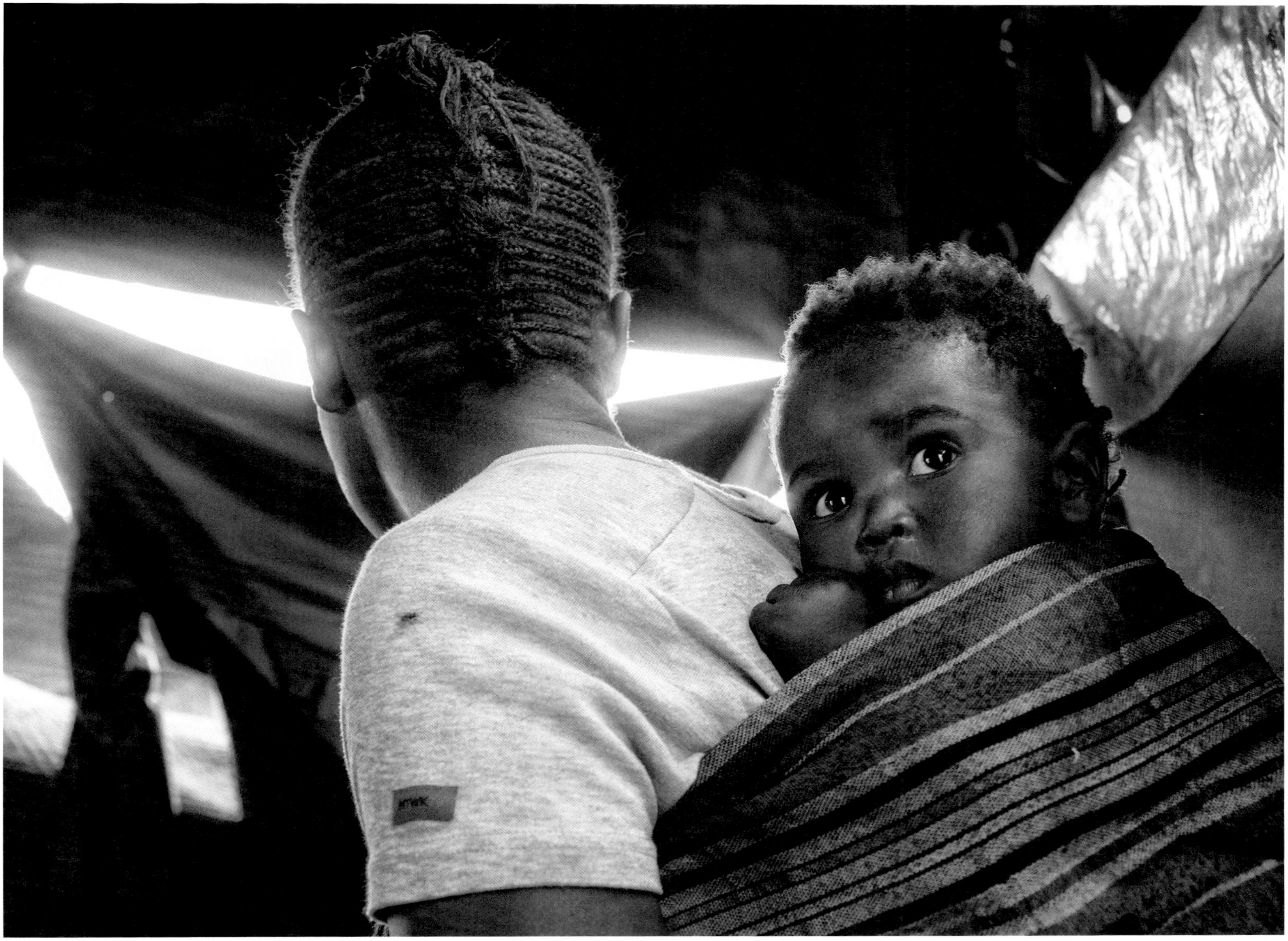

A resident of the Village visits Donald (August 2017)

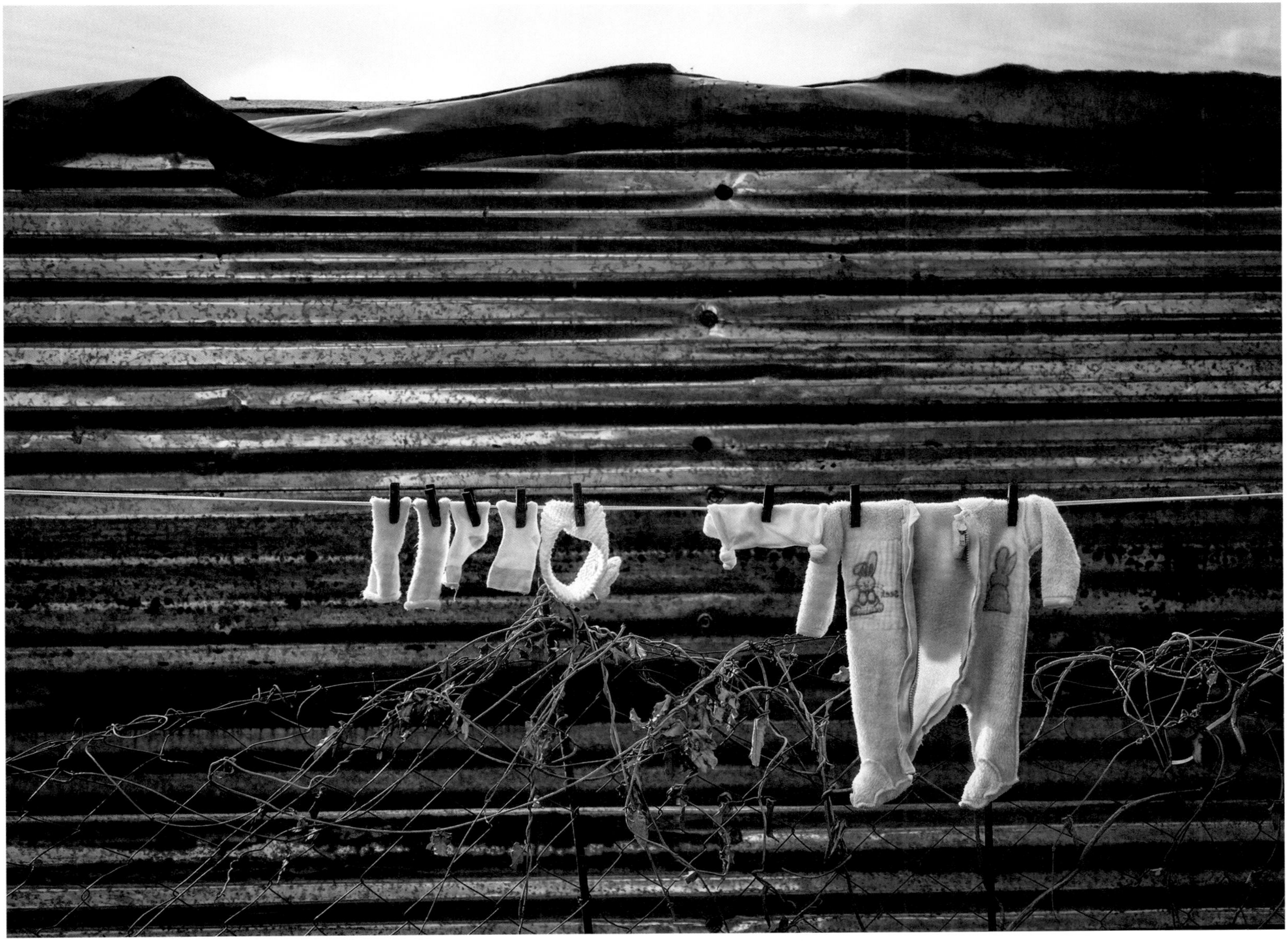

Laundry dries across the lane from Donald's stand (August 2017)

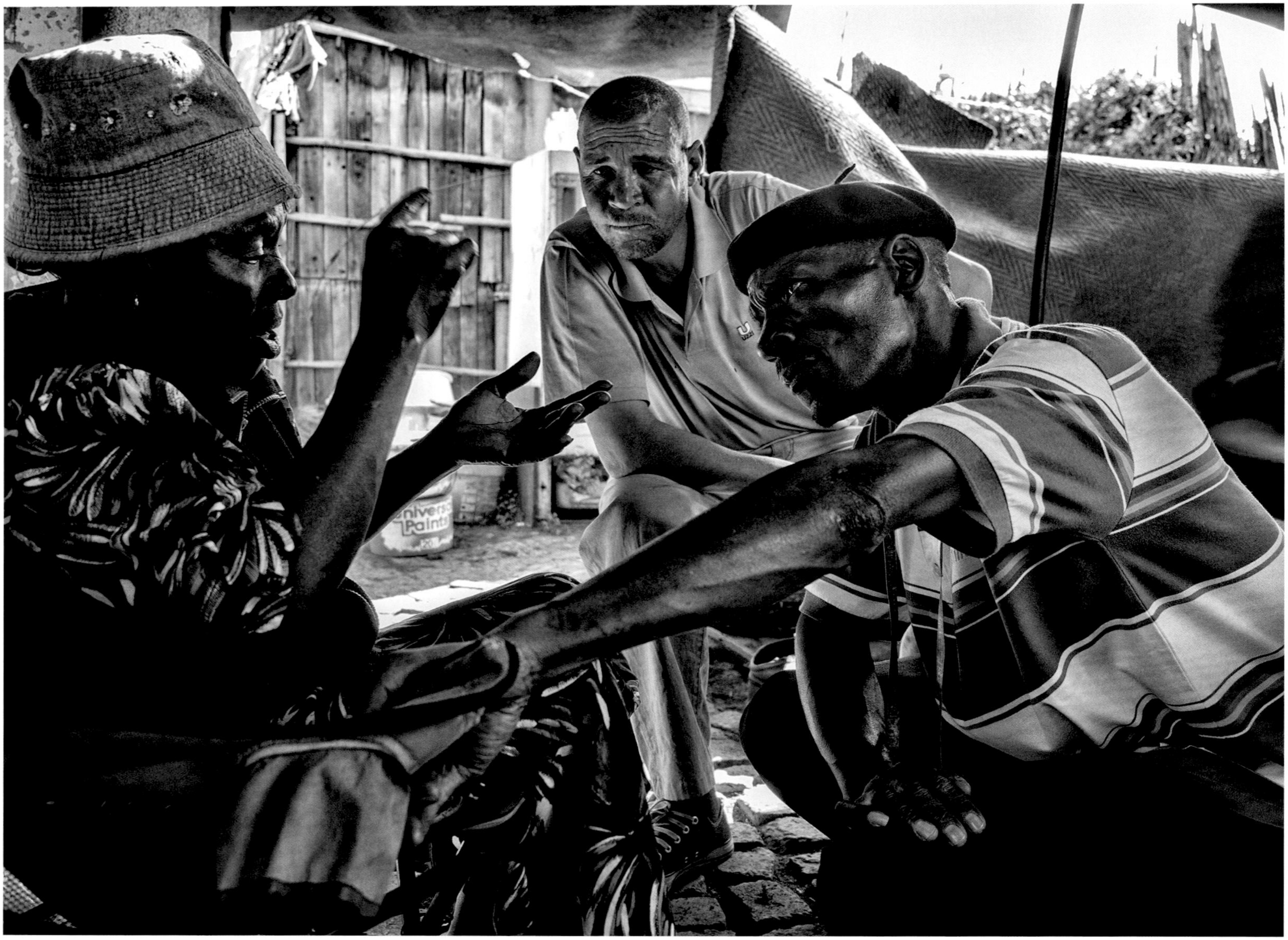

Donald provides counsel to a neighbor (September 2016)

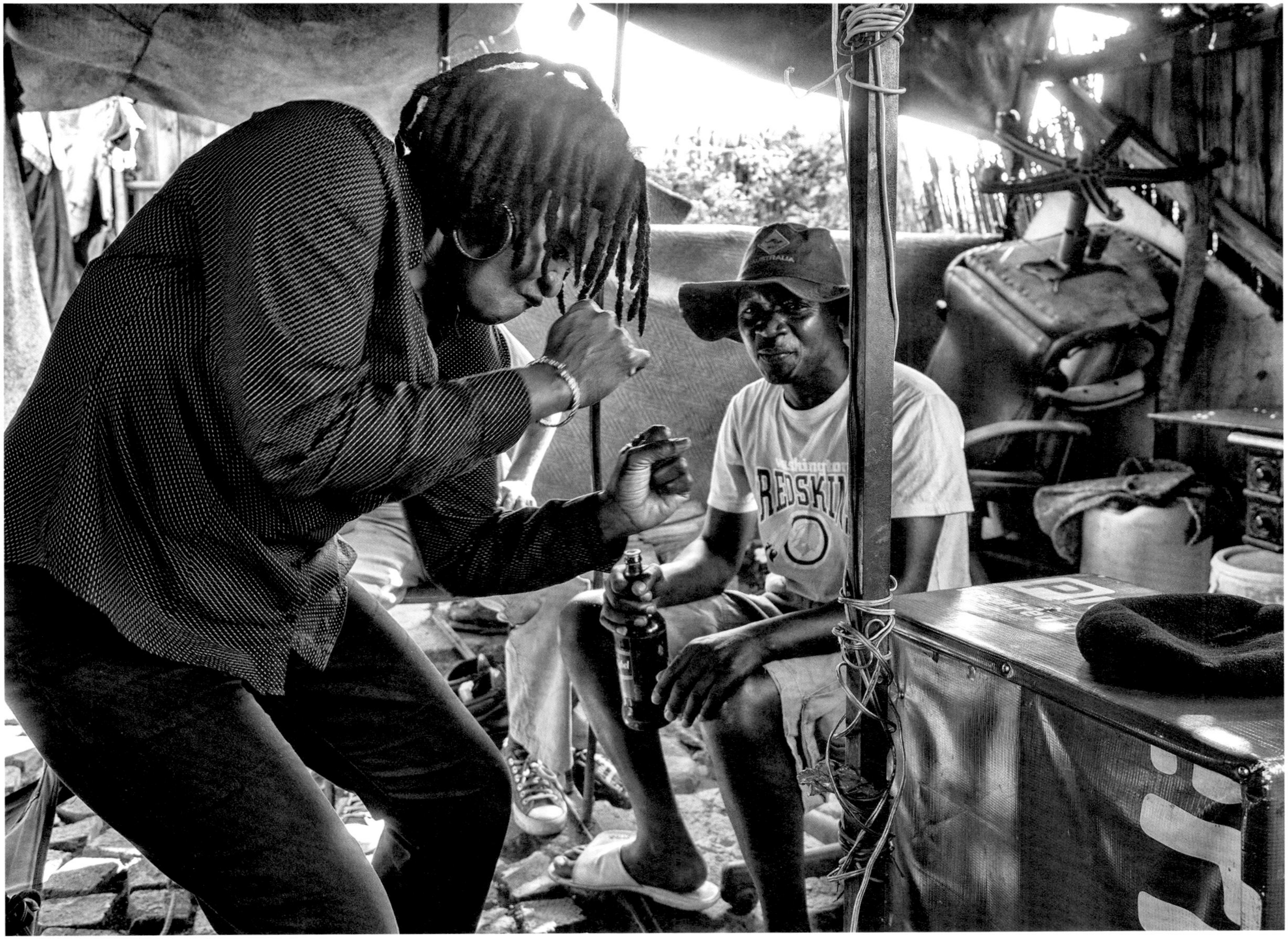

Home is where the music is (September 2016)

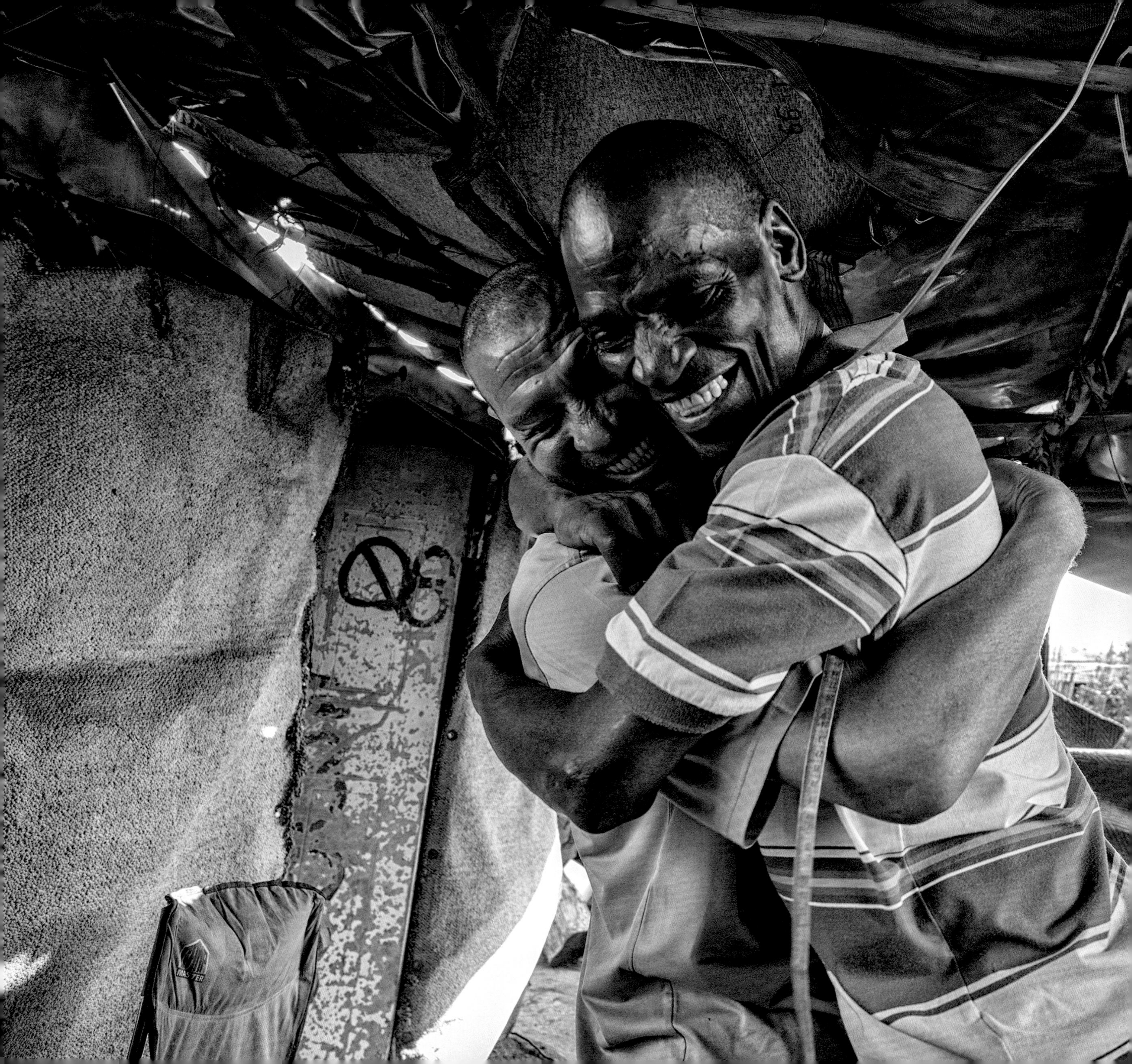
MASTER

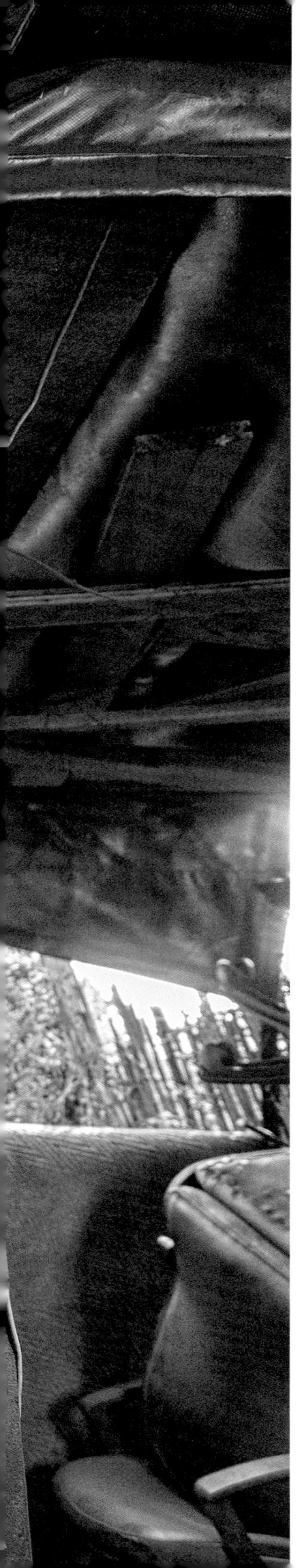

Donald and Allie embrace
(August 2016)

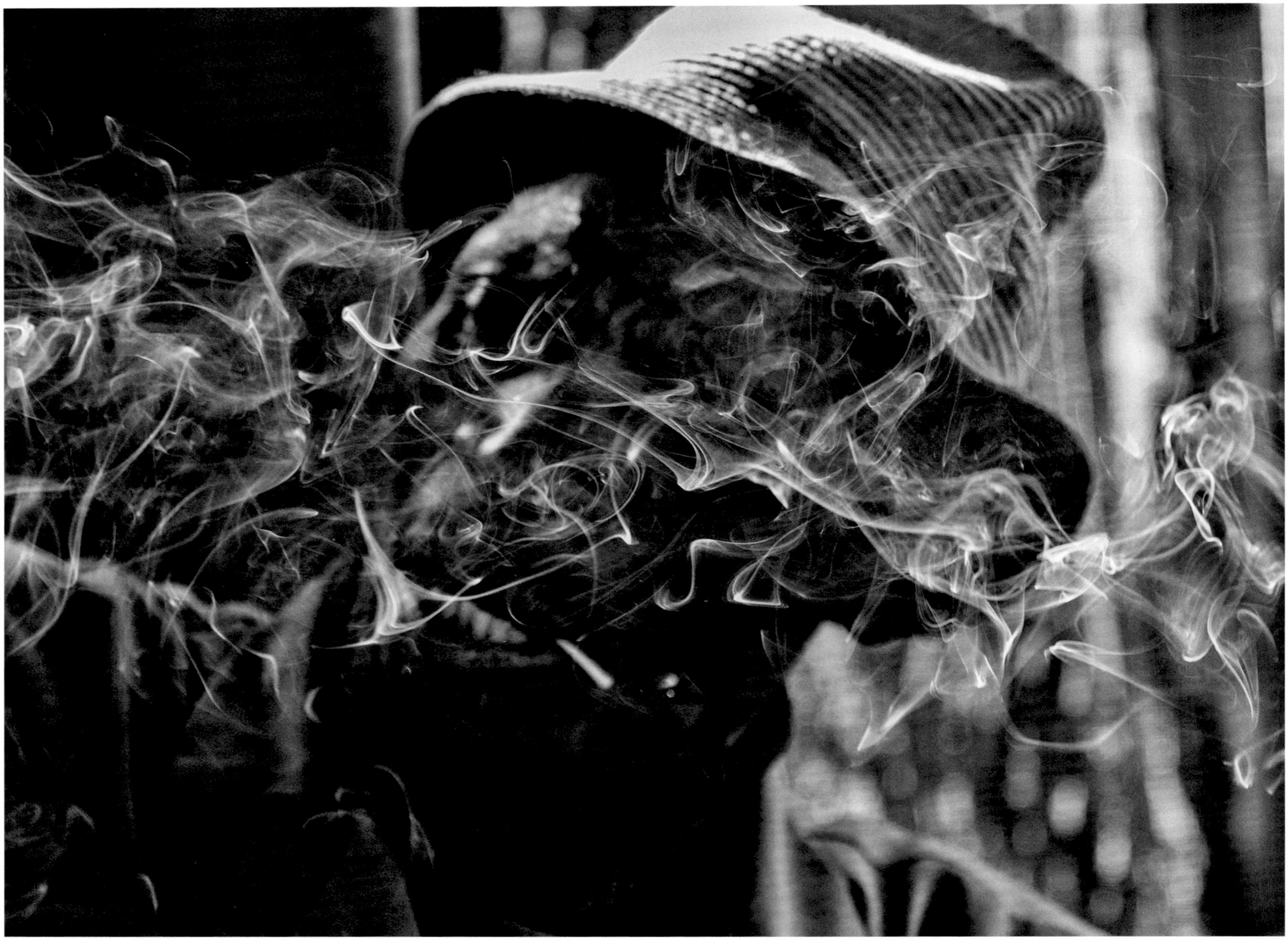

"Life is a compendium of wonders" —Donald (August 2017)

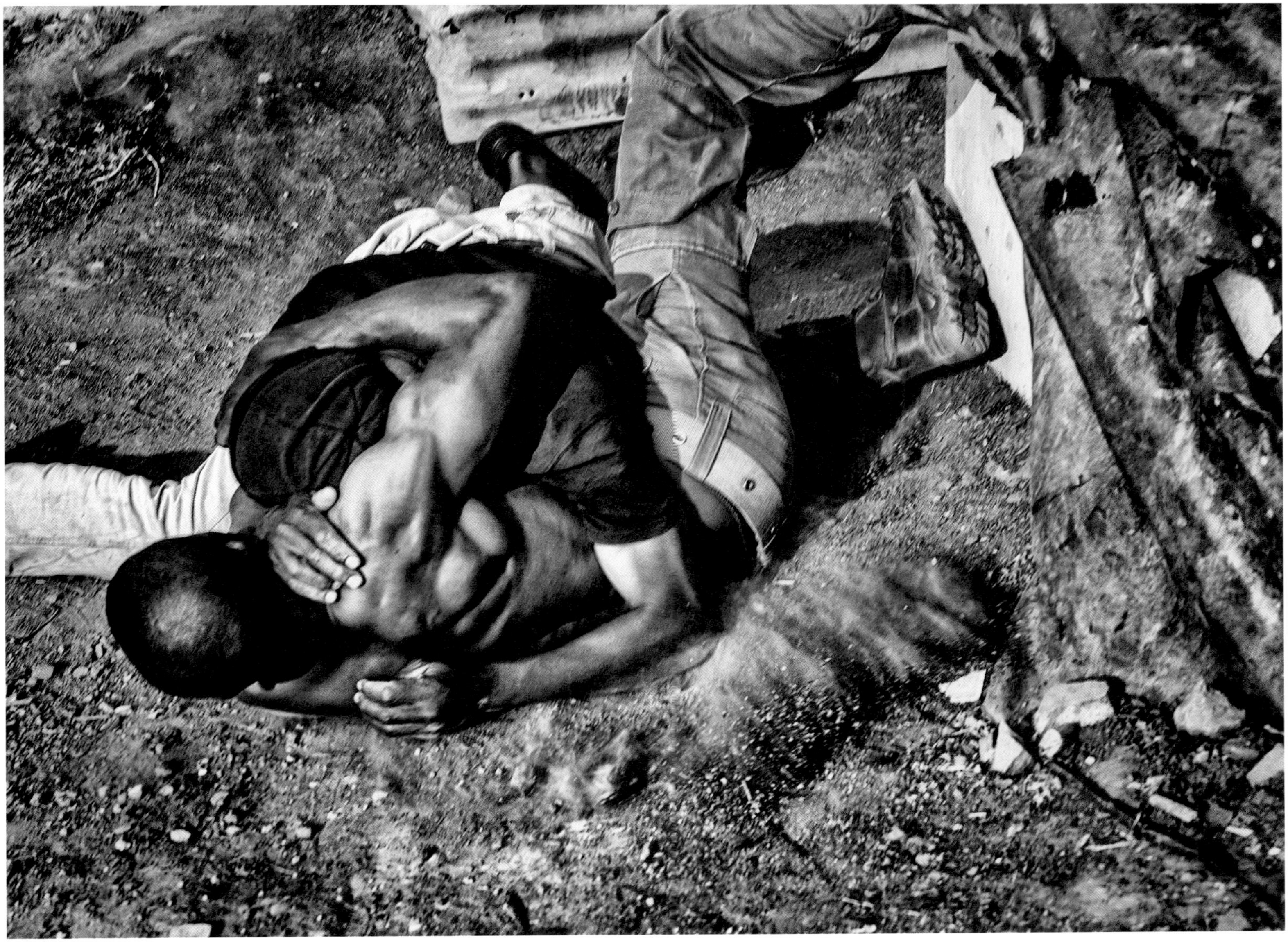

Scuffle on a Saturday afternoon (September 2017)

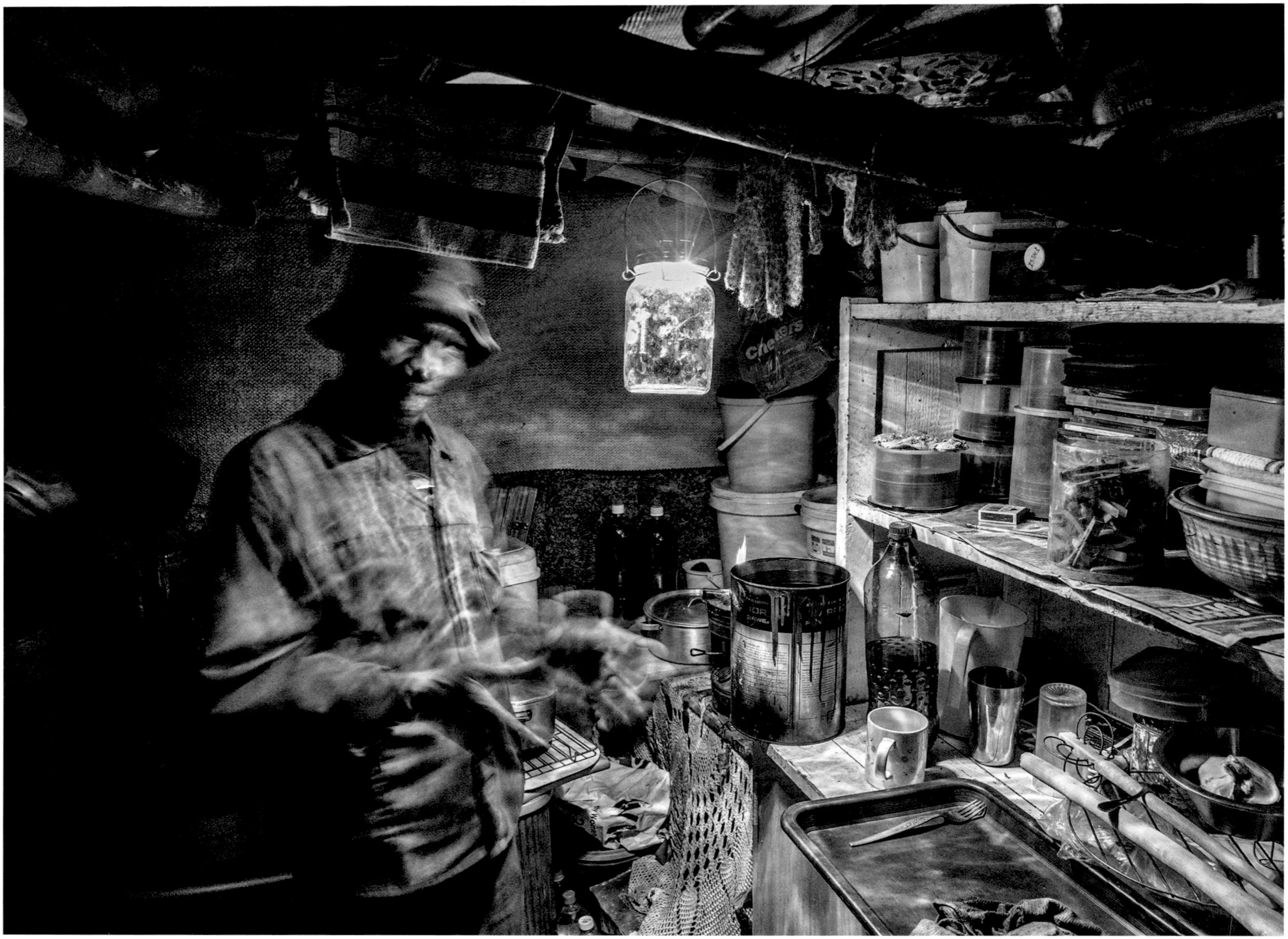

Donald prepares a meal in his shack (September 2017)

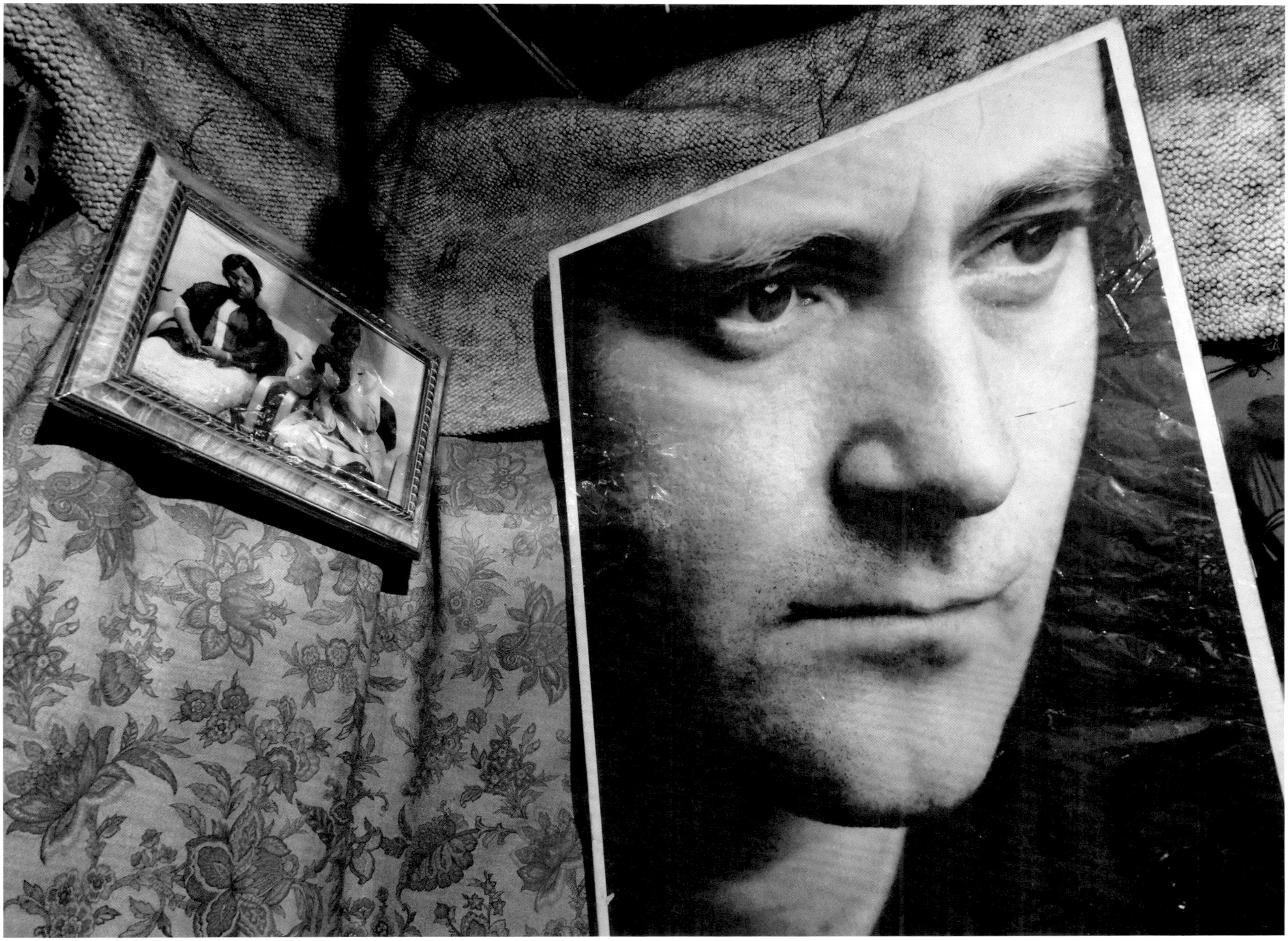

Donald's bedroom with a wedding picture and a poster for the Phil Collins song "Another Day in Paradise" (September 2017)

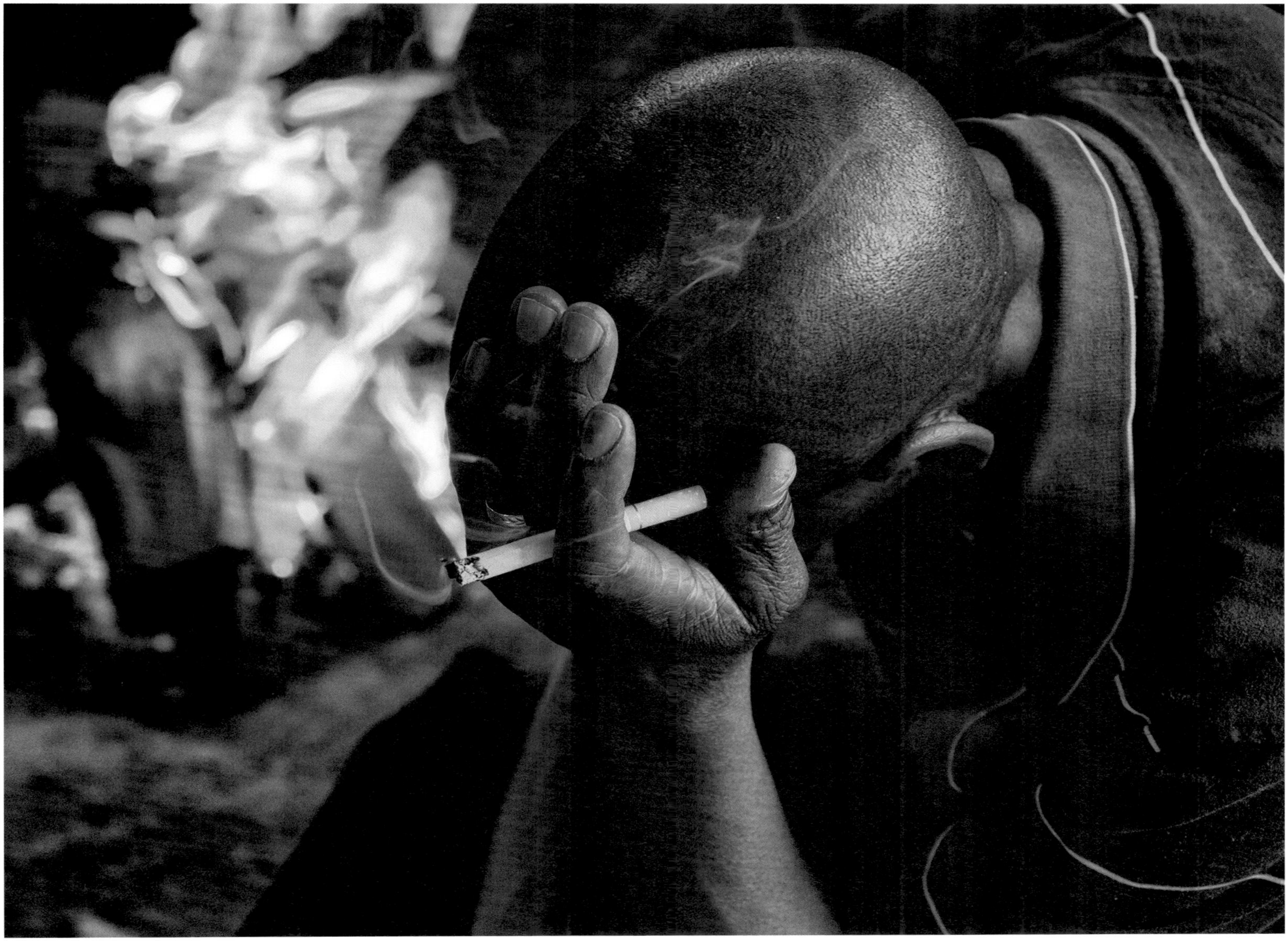

A moment of stillness (September 2017)

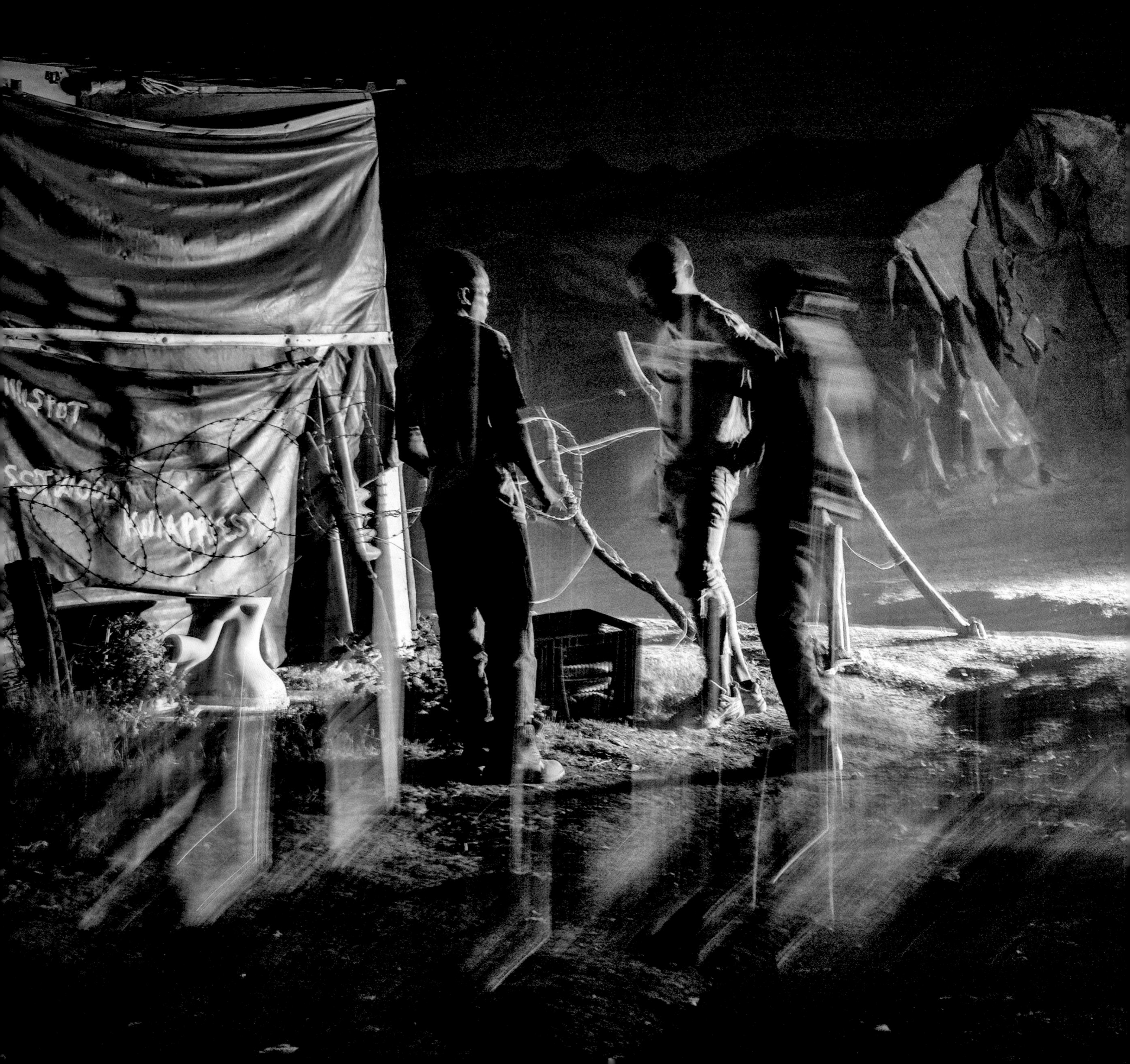

A gathering illuminated
by passing headlights
(September 2017)

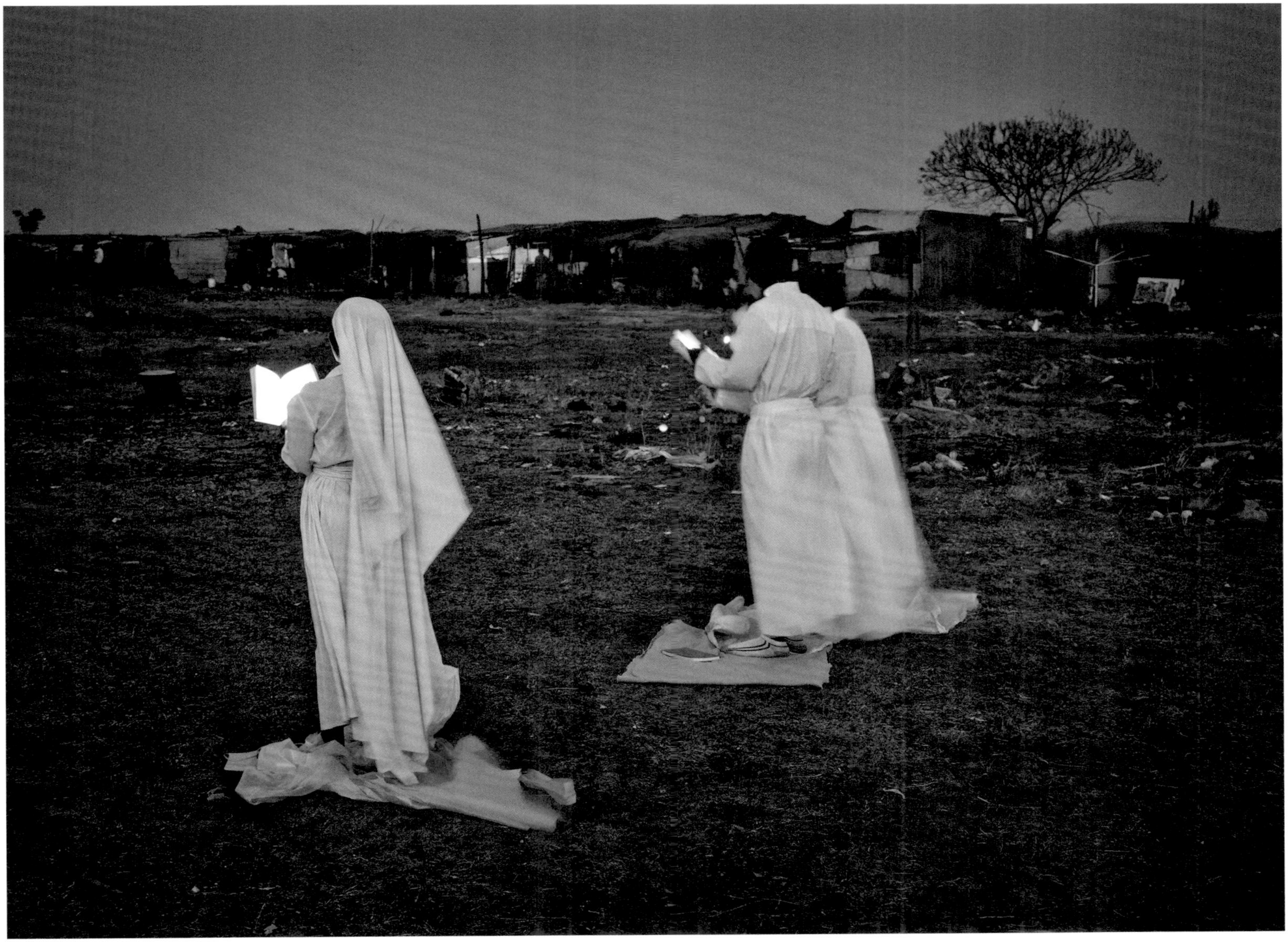

Evening gospel #2 (September 2017)

Life is a "compendium of wonders." It is this mixed thing. It keeps on rolling. You think you know it all and then you get to the other side and you find it is something else. And then you turn it around and you find it is something else again. It gives you many reflections of itself. That is why I say life is a compendium of wonders.

—Donald Banda

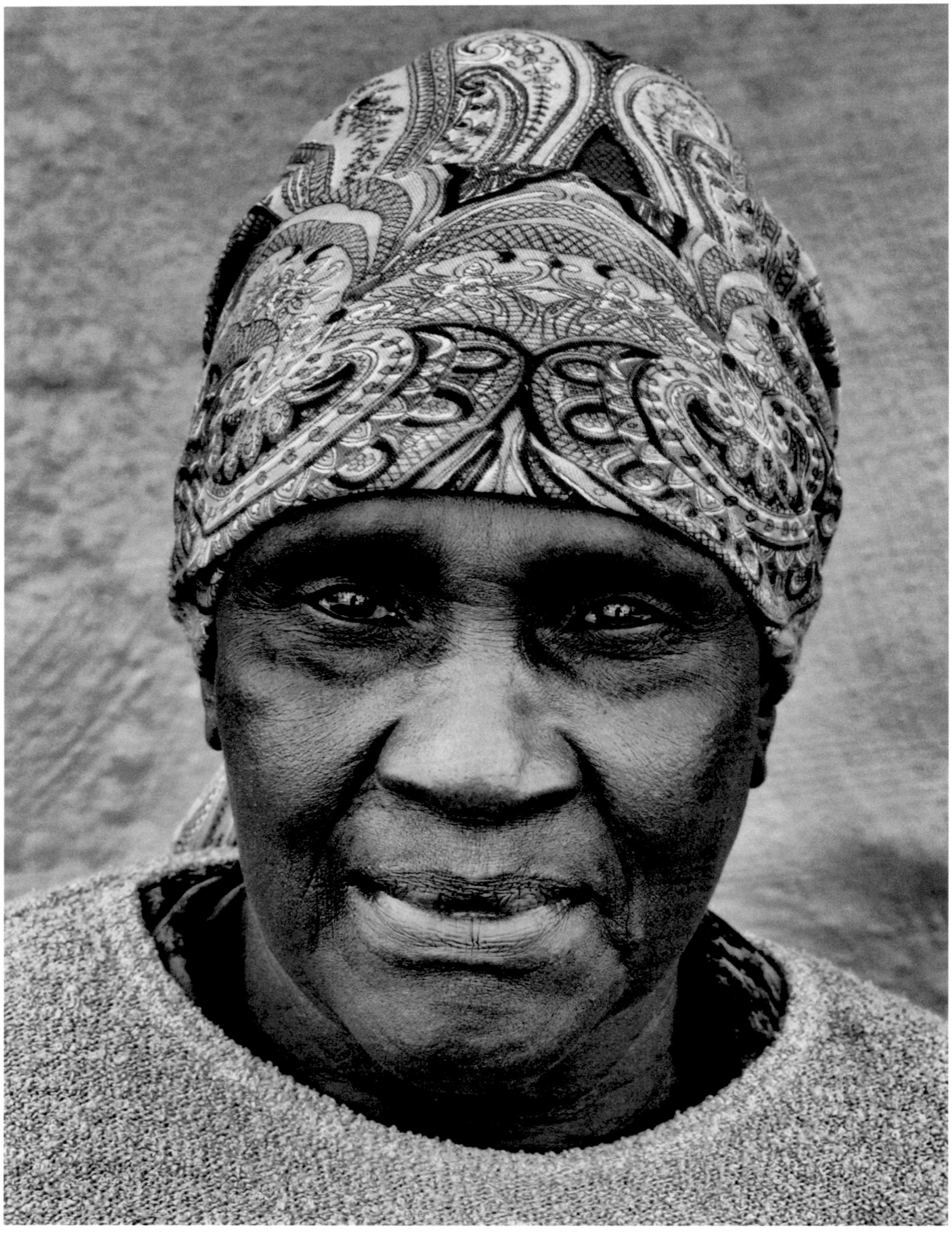

Annah, the mother of Donald (September 2012)

DONALD BANDA

An oral history of home and belonging

I was born in 1960 on the twelfth of December. I am the third oldest in my family. I have a brother and a sister who are ahead of me. My older brother is deceased now. He was murdered around Mooikloof in 1982. Back then it was called *Zwavelpoort*. It was still jungle back then.

So anyway, we moved here by 1968—the same year my brother Christopher was born. We came from a place called *Bophuthatswana*. That's the name. It was the gathering place or homeland for the Tswana people. It is just north of Pretoria and our father built us a house there before he died.

My father worked at the Wingate Park Country Club. He passed away in 1971 after a long illness. We buried him in Mamelodi. We were still young then. We didn't understand death. As children we could see something was wrong. People were coming from all over. Some were crying and some were throwing tantrums. But as children we didn't know what was happening.

Anyway, as I said, this land was jungle back then. I remember when the reservoir was built out on those hills. You know the one that looks like a wineglass? People worked round the clock to construct it, day and night for two years. And after it was finished, we started seeing roads materializing—a road here, a road there. The cars appeared and then the houses came. It began like a joke, but the changes continued until the land transformed into what you see today.

It was mostly farms out here. One man owned this land before they built those million-rand houses. The whole area running from Checkers to the Garsfontein Extension and all of Mooikloof belonged to him. His cows grazed here. And he employed hundreds of people.

In those days, we knew our neighbors by name. If visitors came by they would say, "I am here to see Mr. So-and-So." And we would reply, "Oh, Mr. So-and-So lives up the road about five kilometres away. Let me take you." And if you arrived late and the sun was setting we would offer you a place to stay for the night. We would welcome you. We would give you warm water to wash your feet. We would slaughter a chicken to fill your belly. And in the morning we would walk with you.

But this spirit is gone now.

* * *

Gone are the days of the night vigils and the honoring of the dead. In my youth, people from all over gathered for a wake. They showed respect with silence. They brought their condolences, strengthening one another with the verses of the departed. You know, bandaging the wounds of the grieving, so they could heal.

"The Gods have given; the Gods have taken."

"When God closes one door another one opens."

But as time passed, some people failed to attend the night vigils. They wouldn't share words of support. They wouldn't give donations to the family. They wouldn't partake in the feasts.

They forgot we all wear the same blanket. We all experience sickness and frailty. We all die. And in this forgetting, they soon discovered that when tragedy befell their family, only a handful of people showed up. Some bore witness, but few shared in the feast. The cow was butchered, but the beef was wasted.

But we can safeguard against this by lending a hand to our neighbors. In this way, we become a community. But trust me, if we fail to support one another, the meat will be squandered. One man alone cannot eat a whole cow. It will rot. And you will find that even if you take the meat out in wheelbarrows the beggars on the street will not eat it.

This is how we are living in this world of ours.

* * *

In our culture wherever your relatives are buried is your home. It is your place. And if you have worries or a heavy heart, you would go and sit by your ancestors' graves: your grandfathers or great-grandfathers. You know, just taking your worries out there. And even if you're just sitting there silently and not even saying your prayers aloud, you would feel better. You would come away blessed. This is how we lived.

But now those burial places are white man's land. And we have nowhere to go with our worries. They have built big houses out here. And the owners would never believe that their properties sit where once were graves, because whatever was there previously was demolished and replaced with new landscaping and greens. And everything is neat and orderly.

Look out there! I had family all over. I was born out here. My grandfather was here. My uncles and aunts lived in Mooikloof. Look! All of my family were here and now all of them are in Mamelodi, Soshanguve, Mpumalanga, Moloto, everywhere. We are scattered and we don't even have the time to visit one another.

* * *

Things turned upside down after my father's death. I was still a young man. I had to find ways to support my family and me. And the ways I chose were not good ways. I chose bad ways. Although for me, they were good because they put bread on the table. It was kind of a joke. You know? I was doing my things but eventually my problems caught up with me.

I went to jail for a long time. I lost twenty years of my life, because of this gangster thing. And when I came out, I didn't recognize the world.

My siblings were still children when I left and when I returned they were adults with their own children. Even today, people are always wondering, "Why do you only have one child? Your younger brothers and sisters have three or four children and you only have one!"

They don't understand. There is no making children in jail.

And when I was released from prison, I found the jungle was no more.

I came back to find a town where once there had only been fields and bushes. Look around you. It grows to be this town where I don't even know which street to go, but I was born here. Because the jungle, it just crossed that way and that way and that way. Now it is a town, but I don't know which street is which, because it was planned by somebody who didn't even know what the jungle was.

* * *

To make a long story short, in my criminal days I specialized in home burglaries. I would look for specific things: jewelry and other expensive stuff. You know like those watches with the blue dolphins on them. I would not ransack the place. I would not smash it to hell. No! That was not my way. I was so selective that people would think the stuff was misplaced—not stolen. And I didn't resort to violence. If the homeowner returned unexpectedly I would slip away. I was an escape artist, an *ontsnapper*.

I was very good at what I did. And I felt justified in my actions, because I believed I was taking back from the white man what had been taken from me. I hated the white man for his arrogance and greed. You know, he acted superior to us. And we cowered like dogs to him: "*Ja, baas. Nee, baas. Goed, baas. Ekskuus, baas.*"[1]

I gained a reputation for avoiding incarceration. In the early days, before my imprisonment, I could break out of a police station before the fingerprinting. I was out. Running was in my blood.

But it wasn't until I was locked up that I discovered I was *Ngangelizwe*. I would run until "I am as big as this world." That's where the name *Ngangelizwe* comes. I will run until *I am as big as this world*. You will find me nowhere.

I was the leader of the Air Forces. The Air Forces are the guys who "run" in jail, the ones who escape. We deal only with escaping.

You should know there are the Big Five. Those we call the dogs, because they work with the police in jail. The Big Five. They eat extra food. That is their reward.

And then we have the Twenty-Sixes, the ones who deal with drugs and robbery. And then we have the Twenty-Sevens. Their flags are plain red with no other color. The Twenty-Sevens are the guys who deal with blood. If I hate you enough I can buy them with a packet of tobacco. They are going to kill you. Dead. The Twenty-Sevens deal only with blood.

And the Twenty-Eights. The Twenty-Eights are the owners of the jail. They call jail "home." The Twenty-Eights are the ones who rape because they take the other men and make them wives. That is the Twenty-Eights now.

And that is when I found out that I am *Ngangelizwe*. You know this gangsterism thing. How does it work? Let's say you are kind of like 3,000 gang members. You will never know one another, all of you. But if one of you does something wrong, it takes all of you down. So one thing you should know . . . let's say that somebody who is your brother by number stabbed somebody yesterday and you don't know because you are not mixing with them, you are keeping aside, but you have the number. Those guys they need to stab you back or kill you back if there is a killing.

---

[1] Yes, boss. No, boss. Good, boss. Sorry, boss.

Because this stabbing of the people of number is a demeaning act. There is this thing called, "*Jy moet die bloed gaan haal.*" You must go and fetch the blood or take it back. If you don't take it back you should remember: you have a *number.*

So if it is me, an Air Force Three, and I am being stabbed by a Big Five, I have only two days to decide. On the third day, I must go and stab back in order to be on my same position. And if it is a Big Five he has four days. The fifth day if it passes don't even think about it. Don't go beyond your number. It won't work. You work towards your number.

Even if you are alone, one man, you are representing all your brothers. That is how it works. There is no excuse. That is why if you get to die, you just get to die. Number is a stupid thing, because it doesn't ask you. It *calls* you.

And I tell you, for all those years, that is when I saw that God is really great. Trust me. You are just standing there! People are being hurt. Some are being killed. Nothing touches you. Nothing. That's when I knew, "I am not alone here." Something big is protecting me. It will only be blood. It is your blood. And the other one's blood. Not my own. Some people are losing ears, eyes, noses, hands. Look some are dying. I am just standing there. But I am not getting hurt. Now, I am not talking about once. I am talking for all those years. Now, that was something. Wow! This is something.

* * *

THE STORY OF NGANGELIZWE

They call this "the beginning." Or you can call it "the beginning and the end." They say there were ten guys at the beginning. And these ten guys were the ones who were talking about things. Like you and I are doing right now.

Among these ten, there was this guy called Ngangelizwe, which means "as big as the world." That's me.

Now I am giving you the picture of how it came about. There were only these ten people and they were talking about fixing the community. "We should do this and that." And whatever they agreed upon, they did.

But there was this guy, the Number Ten guy. He was always disagreeing. Whatever they talked about he said, "No." He came up with reasons for not voting for this and that. They even challenged him by saying, "What is with you? Why do you always question whatever we are suggesting?"

So they started talking about building a school.

"What is a school?" the tenth guy asked.

"A school is a place where we can educate our children."

"No, no, I think a school is good."

And at another meeting, they discussed building a hospital. Now in Zulu we call this "*umtholampilo*," which means "the place that gives life."

"What is a hospital?" the Number Ten guy asked.

"You! You always stand in front of the uplift-ment of the community. What is it about you?"

"No, I want to know. I'm not going to agree if I don't know."

"A hospital is where you are healed if you are sick or injured."

"Are you telling me if I am going to die and I visit the hospital they will stop my death?"

"No, no! They can't do that. If you get to die, you get to die. But if you can be saved, you will be saved."

"Oh, I understand," he said. "Umthol-ampilo is good! It can go with the school."

And then at another meeting they discussed building a jail.

"No. What is a jail?"

"You, you, you! You've got many problems. Whenever we speak you interrupt us. A jail is where we house people who are doing wrong."

"Ha! Now, you tell me that my cows will stay in your *kraal*?" he replied. "I don't think so!"

"Ja, if we get them and we lock them up, they will stay."

"No, I don't think so. They will break the place apart and run away, because they don't belong there."

"Since you have such a big mouth, let's start with you and show you what jail is like!"

So they took that guy and locked him inside this tiny little room, kind of like a toilet.

"Ja, now we will see what you will do," they laughed.

Now you should remember that those nine guys put him in jail. They became known as the police. And now we call them the Number Nines, the Nines.

Now they became the police on top of the Number Ten guy. So they say that on the first day Ngangelizwe's heart was green. Green. They brought him food, but he refused to eat. He just looked at the food. And on the second day, his heart was red. Again they brought him food, which he didn't eat. On the third day, they say that his heart was white—white, because on that day Ngangelizwe took the spoon they provided him and started scratching at the brickwork until he opened a hole and ran away.

"I will run until I am as big as the world. You will find me nowhere," he said.

And that's where Ngangelizwe comes from.

* * *

I hated jail. Prison is no place for the faint-hearted. Trust me. I was arrogant because I thought I knew everything. In life, things work against you when you assume you know it all. It takes time to learn.

Now the funny part is that some people don't even get a chance to learn because they die outright. I will tell you like this. There was this young guy. We grew up together. So this young guy was fascinated with our lifestyles. One day he decided to accompany one of my friends into town. Now this guy was living at location and this was the first time he visited town. Just here in Elardus Park he was shot dead. Shot dead, the first time he came to town. Just for his troubles, because he was fascinated by the lives we lived. It is funny.

* * *

Man, I don't know what I was thinking back then. I was mixed up. I only cared about self and the things coming my way. And the funny part is I knew it was bad. I have a great mother who was trying by all means to tell me.

"Son, what is it with you? What do you want in life? If it's damage you are looking for, you will find it. You have to change your ways, because you are going too far."

In prison I started to understand and respect her words. I got the drift of what my old lady was saying. It was not for me to cry to her for help, because she would have told me one thing.

"My son, didn't I say you were going astray? Didn't I say so?"

Now, I did her a favor—a big favor—and she respects me for it. Not *once* did I ask for her sympathy or support.

She was not to blame for my poor choices.

* * *

Trust me when one door closes another one opens. We might miss the opportunity because we concentrate on the closed one. There is no way all the doors can be closed while you are alive. If all the doors are closed then you are dead. But while you are breathing, trust me, a door is going to open up. It might be somebody coming along and asking, "Hey man! Why are you sitting there lonely?"

That's the door opening. You are still alive. So don't die before you die. Die when you are dead.

That is why I say life is a "compendium of wonders." It is this mixed thing. It keeps on rolling. You think you know it all and then you get to the other side and you find it is something else. And then you turn it around and you find it is something else again. It gives you many reflections of itself. That is why I say life is a compendium of wonders.

* * *

I take responsibility for my decisions. I am my own man. Nobody can buy me. I have always been this odd guy who goes my own way. I do not follow the crowd. I am not going to say, "Okay, you are right" simply because I am outnumbered or intimidated. No! I will say, "You are wrong!" Even if you hurt me, I will cry out, "You are wrong!" So you would know you are mistaken. And the funny thing is if I know I am wrong, I will not accept you saying I am right. I will not take it. I believe in my own truth. And I will not adopt your *plansenyana* unless I can see them working for me. But should they make sense I will borrow them to fit my needs. Trust me, I will take your ideas if they are helpful to me.

* * *

I was afraid of fights as a young boy. In jail, I learned to resort to violence, because it is the only language people understood out there. Only fighting is comprehended. You have to fight back!

And if you are ambushed, you don't cry to the guards that somebody hurt you. No, even if you are covered with blood, you tell the authorities you fell. You lie. You stay put. And then your attackers will be wondering why you are not running away.

Before too long, even before you are stitched up, you go out and hit them the way they hit you. That's the only way they will understand you are a man. You can stand on your own. And that's when you get respect.

Now, that friend I was telling you about. He was really mean. And look, we were not big guys. No! We were big in the head and in the deeds, but we were not big guys. We were kind of like skinny. But we could do our stuff. We were good in what we did. And we didn't do stuff only when we were together. No! Happy can do his stuff. And I can do my stuff. He just had to show his face at the window and say, "Don! Do it!" And I am doing it.

That's how we trusted one another. And even today, we can't change that. We really caught on to one another. I don't know how it happened. But in all of the thousands of people I met it is only that guy. Even now that's how it is. He is like a brother to me.

* * *

"Number has a mind and a life of its own. Number by itself can kill you. There are many people who have laid down their spirits for Number. In Number there is no talk without action. In Number, you talk now, you act now. Number is alive. It has done wonders and it has done countless damage."[2]

* * *

I was arrested in 1974 and was sent to New Lock prison. We were crammed into a holding cell. We slept three or four to a bed.

In the night somebody wet the blankets. When we woke we were soaked in urine and no one could identify the culprit. And then we got the beating of a lifetime.

"Why you pee? You bastard! You bastard!"

After that experience I realized, "Hey, this place is real shit. Shit like shit. It stinks." I tried to avoid that place as best as I could, but I couldn't do so forever. So I went out there again. Now, the second time I was locked up, I started thinking, "Why are these people acting like they were born here? Plastered and painted with this place. What can I do in order for me to be the same?" Ah, trust me, I wasn't like them. I was worse than them. They got to fear me more than I feared them.

It was simple. It was all in my mind—all in my doing. You got to do stuff that others will puke when they see you do. Kind of like, people are sitting there, maybe fifteen, twenty people, sitting there and one of them is pestering you because he has all these friends. He is just agitating you because he has protection and you're alone.

Now what I did in order for me to be recognized, I just acted like I was afraid. But one thing that I did, you see that brick? That brick? I put a piece of that brick in a double or triple sock. And then I relaxed like it was nothing. But whenever the jail is closed they are sitting there, all of them, in a group. I told myself that I am going to hurt that one more than I can hurt anyone. I am going to smack him to hell and back. So, I am taking that sock and I am making it short. I am wrapping it in

[2] See also Human Rights Watch 1994 for a description of the prison conditions in South Africa at the time of Donald's incarceration. This includes a fascinating overview of the number gang system.

my hand like so. I am just hitting back, whichever way I can. You don't make it long. It will end up striking you. You make it short, kind of short, like a short string. Don't make it long. And then after I did that I just started strolling, you know. They are sitting there by the hallway, all of them, looking the other side and making jokes, "Ha ha!" But I know who is my guy, so I am just taking a stroll, going down there, up there, many times over so that they put it in their mind that I am just going up and down.

But there will come a time when I am going to go out there and grab my enemy and I am going to work him in front of his friends. And I am alone. Remember, I am alone!

I am going to make sure they have just made their bed and me, I didn't make my bed. Because I know if I retaliate, the guards will remove me. So my bed is wrapped up. Everything I need to take with me is tied in a bundle.

Now when the time comes I am just making that stroll up, down, up, down . . . when my time comes I just go straight at him. It is all blood spitting. Look, those who are outside, they can't stand up! Blood is working power. Blood has power. They are just being splattered by blood and they just sit there, because anyone who stands up will be struck. Because I am standing up. I just hit and hit. And when I hit I tell him, "You don't shit me! Because I will shit you more." And I am hitting hard!

AIR FORCE THREE—BY THE NUMBERS

1. I don't have anything in the jail.
My kingdom is outside.

2. I die where my brother dies. Wherever my brother's bone falls I will follow.

3. Day and night, I am reading the wind.

4. I always identify with my own kind.

5. I cannot bring poison to my brother.

* * *

And everyone knows it was my deed alone. I did it myself. And so, everyone is scared of you, because you hit the first one, and you hit the second one, and the third one! But it is only a trick of the mind. Simple. Ha ha! And after that you can just pull your hat over your eyes and take a nap. And they will never know if you are awake or asleep. Then you can take four or five hours to recuperate. So you are surviving! That's how you should do your stuff, because if you don't fend for yourself, you're in for a hard one. Oh, you're in for a hard one!

So even if you sleep, you bark, "Hey!" And they jump, because they know you can act. And you don't lose it. You just always do the stuff. And that's how me and Happy lived.

And sure, we were feared and hated. But the people couldn't question what we did because we did it in order for us to survive. And we were the backbone of the *Ngangelizwe* thing. Everything that happens anywhere they would come to us.

Trust me, whether I was alone or with Happy, we made sure we had an answer for them. And we always answered appropriately, because we had the book. And in the answers, there can be three ways in which you can solve stuff. We had a rule book. It was in our heads. So that's how simple it was for us. We were hated by the police and by the other gangs, but we survived. We survived where nobody thought we could.

* * *

Home is where I feel comfortable. Wherever I lay my hat, that's my home. As long as it is not under force, that's my home.

If I find myself among mad people, I will pretend to also be crazy. Because this is how we live. If you are not mad, you are dead. So if the people around you are mad, you must feign madness. Or you must act wilder than them, because that's the only way they'll recognize you as a human being.

Tell me, if all the people are dirty and you arrive in a clean white suit, will they accept you? No! They will come with their sweaty hands and grab you all over. And by the end of the day, you will be filthier than them. You must be like them. The same applies here.

Look, the people are teaching you. You might come to the place a good guy and law-abiding citizen, but you find out all the time at the corner, you get the *klap* (slap). You must decide whether you should be like them or worse. Because if you always cower, you will be eaten alive. Trust me.

* * *

You can trap the body. But you cannot trap the mind. In my days before prison, if I ate food I would always wrap a little up for later, for self or others. Little packets of food for later.

In prison, when my body ached from hunger I would go back to the memory of these little packets and my stomach would be full. Or I would grab a cold beer from twelve years back, you know. And often, I would travel to places I have only read about. Far away. And I would be free. Free as in "free."

* * *

I realized I have this capacity to think and to make sense of right and wrong when I was in prison. I started questioning the world, especially the life of prison, "What is going on here? No, I can do better than this."

You can incarcerate the body, not the mind. Trust me, for what it is worth, not the mind. The mind is going wherever it wants. You can go to America whilst you are incarcerated. You can go to India. It's only up to you to give it a try. So that's what I did. And lucky enough, I discovered reading. Books are my life. They made me. Even though I didn't go to school, I started to understand the world through reading.

* * *

I never went back to jail after I got out in 1997. Never. I moved in with my sister in Mamelodi for a while. When I first got out of prison, I got some contract work and rented a place. But you know the problem with temporary jobs. They are unreliable and you might find yourself only be employed for three or four months. So I decided to go to my sister's place. And while I was living there I ran a tailoring business on the side. I had this Singer sewing machine.

It was not a walk in the park, man. It was sad. Because I tried to be on my own. But at the same time, now if you know you are working contracts. You are tiling for six months. You are making good money. But for three years you are not working. So that money of six months can't afford you for three years. So it means you are going back to I don't know where. . . .

* * *

So I am good at this sewing thing. Real good. There was this time I saw a woman on the train with ripped trousers.

"Hey, look! Look your zip is torn," I said.

"Hey, how did you see that?"

"You don't have to worry. I make fashion."

"No, no, what were you looking at?"

"No, that's my nature. I am looking. Come here."

In the train, I was sewing and she was standing there. I got the call because I carried the needle and thread with me. So I just stitched it up for free right there and then.

And the bystanders were saying, "Wow, this man is doing it."

"Yes! Don't worry that I am looking at your crotch or something. Because I am the fashion man, yes."

"How did you see that?"

"No, it is my nature. It is in me. I am looking where you can't look."

* * *

I have lived in the camp for several years now. Early on we stayed in makeshift shelters. In the morning, we would wrap up our plastic and our belongings and put them in a hole before going to work. Because if the metro police spotted our stands they would come and break them down. They would burn us out. It ended up that even Charles Nqakula, the Minister of Safety and Security, was fined about R10,000 to rebuild what the police had destroyed. Because Colin and Denise Dredge were now fighting with their lawyers, "These people are homeless so you can't just burn their shelters." And they won the matter in court and they told Nqakula to pay. He didn't pay and the matter was taken to Bloemfontein. And out there by Bloemfontein that's where they charged him kind of like R10,000. But eventually, it came to the point where they decided to build this camp to control the living. And then the people started living out here.

Man, it was bad. If you know what bad means. It was real bad, because we were living out here. There were no guarantees, you might be going out and leaving your tarp in the hole, your food and whatever . . . and when you come back somebody had stolen your stuff. And it was an everyday occurrence. And sometimes you would be forced to live from one hole to another. You would put your stuff here today and then tomorrow the police would come and chase you away. Every day from one hole to another.

They would usually find us. Because you should know that even if it is jungle wherever a person is walking, the trail is starting to show. You might use different trails, but at the end of the day they will always point the same direction. That's how you will know there are people out there. You might find fifteen paths that all lead to the same place. The trail will always sell you out.

* * *

Look, I am talking about children being born in holes like snakes. It has happened here—people living in holes. You are walking through the scrubland and you hear a child's cry. You look up, thinking the noise is coming from the trees. You are mistaken because they are underground. Someone has dug a hole and scattered dirt around to conceal the spot. And unless you know how to read the signs, you will stroll right by without noticing. Only the sounds will be evident.

Here you will find children who have been raised in holes in the jungle. When they say "home," they are referring to this place. And when this land is turned into a suburb and they no longer have a home, they will dig another hole in another jungle. That's how people live.

* * *

In this camp, people are living in groups according to their understandings: me and you here. That is how we live and interact. We are in groups. In a way we are a community. But like I told you, we rarely intervene on each other's behalf. One day you may hear me crying. Will you knock on my door? No.

We are not good neighbors. Neighbors should be caring and loving, because you should try to be the neighbor you would like to have. So meaning, you should take responsibility. You know, not doing to others what you don't want done to you.

Now, it doesn't apply here, because everybody is in the mind-set to make money. They don't care about anything that gets in their way. It might be a person. It might be a dog, a cat. It should just get the hell out of the way, because they are out for the money. That is the problem of this place. It is not really a community here.

* * *

People are not doing things blindly. They are doing it because they have the knowledge. They have know-how. There are these guys in all locations you find them under the trees. They are seeing. They are planning. They are conspiring, "Oh, this guy is always clean. Where does he work?" They get to plot. And then they see you every day so it might happen that one of the good days after you go, they break into your place and rob you blind. And if by bad luck you are home, they may even hurt or kill you. You will find you have been crippled for such small stuff: a DVD, maybe a flat-screen TV, a leather jacket or a pair of *takkies* (trainers). Look, those takkies might be expensive, but you think that they are going to sell them decently. No! Takkies of R1000 are going to be sold for R50 or a case of beer.

* * *

You know there are people who are killing people for a cigarette. A puff. And I am getting sad finding out somebody is killing somebody for a just puff. Dying and taking the cigarette and then that cigarette pack is bloody. Running and lighting at the same time. And before long he is being caught and go to jail. Remember somebody has just lost his life and you just taken a cigarette that you are not going to even enjoy. It is sad.

* * *

We ran out here to make a life. I mean there is no place like home. But if home no longer feels like home, we are lost. We are a lost generation. That's where we are. I mean it is only the *oh*'s and the *ah*'s all the time. There is no way out of this one.

"Oh, oh, oh!"

"Ah, ah, ah!"

It is like you are wondering what is coming to this world. Wow!

If someone says, "Wow, it's a wonder," he is questioning what happened to life itself. It just evaporated "poof" into thin air like a magician with his trick. It shouldn't work like that.

But now I am getting back to the point where you, as the Bible says, will find things are not as they seem. This indicates the end of the world is upon us. Look what the world has come to. It has gone to the dogs, man. Trust me. The dogs are ruling instead of the people, because when man was created he was given dominion over every animal on Earth. He was the boss, meaning he had the brains. But I doubt this now.

I think we are getting to the point of ruin. Humans have always been destructive. I mean if you find a place unspoiled by human beings, you will see a natural cycle of birth and death. But let humans touch a place and you will find real devastation. I mean the death will be all the way. Humans don't preserve anything. No, we are always kicking things about. We only live for today and we think tomorrow will take care of itself.

* * *

When they built this camp, they took people out of the jungles. Because we were isolated: a group here, a group there. The camp was intended to house the workers. You know, the people looking for jobs or those of us who need to live closer to the jobsites. Or those of us saving money so we can do better for our families.

And in the early days of this camp before the expansion, I lived on the coolest street you could get. The boundary of the settlement used to be right behind my shack. It was peaceful. Everyone knew one another. Then they brought in other people and the dynamics changed. The newcomers didn't give a damn about the laws. And that's when you started to find somebody is taking two stands and he is building such a big house that you can't tell where it begins and where it ends. And that's when the shebeens started multiplying and crime increased. And today you find these liquor establishments, like 519, blaring their music all night long—and with the drinking and the constant ruckus, you find problems.

I think it is going to stay this way forever until they demolish this place. It can't change, because even the police are afraid to tackle the matter. And informing on the troublemakers is dangerous and futile. So most of us have learned to live in silence.

And with these changes came the deaths. You know, when we lived in the bushes you could go years before you heard of someone dying and usually this was of natural causes. But bad things started happening after we moved behind these fences. Somebody burns to death in his shack and people claim it is an accident. They say he was a drunk.

This doesn't just happen. Fire is very painful, man. You can't sit there while you burn out. No! You would be kicking and screaming. But at least four or five people have died here by fire. There was always a quarrel that preceded the blaze—you know, a fight over gambling or over a girl. And then the next morning you hear that guy burned out in his shack.

* * *

"Life goes on. When we die we will be replaced.

It doesn't matter how important we are. The dead are forgotten; only the living are remembered.

This is how it should be.

Even Jesus Christ is only remembered on Sundays."

* * *

So, you will find I am living in this birdcage. That's where I am. And I like it in this birdcage, because you can't just invade it like you want to. You know there is this stone throwing and stuff. But if it comes here, trust me, not even a stone can pass through. You see this mesh and the wires?

You will find that I built my shack real strong. Inside the tarpaulin I put a perimeter of sticks to keep intruders out. You might come to cut the plastic and you will find this barrier. And along the ground you will find a zinc plate that protects against the water. My shack has always been very secure and very dry. No bad people or bad weather can get in, especially when I lock the door and the gate.

* * *

The troubles are overdue. Illegal immigration is changing South Africa. You should know this is happening in many countries. And that's why you find crime is so rife. Not meaning there was no crime before. But now it is bad, because foreigners who don't belong here and don't care about anything are committing the wrongs. They are only here as visitors. So they are getting to do whatever they please.

I will let you know that the people who are born here do not rob others blindly. No, they do it like this. They would rather move from their place of birth and go elsewhere to do mischief. They go where they are not known.

* * *

Yes, life has changed from what it was. It was not always this way. We were good neighbors once. Bit by bit, this spirit eroded. You would remember this revolution thing, you know, people toyi-toying: "Power to the people! Hara hara!" These protests came with a price. The price was too big. Many have died.

To cut the story short, other countries have been liberated long ago and the people from there understand how to work the system. So when a place becomes newly democratic, they come rushing to seize opportunities. They come to exploit the situation, because they know the average person doesn't understand what is going on. Many are being robbed—the rich, the poor, the dumb and blind and all. Everybody needs to get to the top. And those who are at the top need to feel secure in their position, so that's where the crooks come in. And they are slick, man. They don't wear disguises. They come plain and smooth. And they are very humble. You would love them.

So you will find the thefts and the bribes and the swindles. And the poor are taking the brunt of these scams. The illiterate and the poor are getting ripped off on a daily basis and there is nothing they can do about it. Even if they want to, they can't unless they change their situation around this literacy and stuff.

But there is nothing I can do about it. I can't stop it. It just keeps happening and happening and happening—all over again. I mean history repeats itself out here.

* * *

I don't think it is all about the country. It is about the people and the time. That's what I think. For this simple fact, if you know what I am talking about. Some people have every opportunity to be bad and yet they refrain from wrongdoing. And then there are those who grow up in good homes and they turn out bad. So how would you explain that one? Can you tell me what happened?

Look, let's talk about this great man, Mandela. He went out there for twenty-seven years. When he came out of jail, people wanted to kill. They smelled blood. He said, "No! No! You don't have to. No!" You remember the time Chris Hani died. The people were up in arms. Even at the funeral they shot in the air and he calmed them down. And they listened.

* * *

But now again, poverty drives people crazy. Some kill themselves, some become robbers. Look there are individuals who make something of themselves even when they are faced with destitution. You know, collecting tins, and making items that others will buy even though they don't have money. Some take plastic and wood to produce art. They make a living out of nothing.

And yet there are others who just sit down in the face of hunger. They put the blame on top of poverty. This doesn't sound true to me. But this is life. You will never know what sounds true and what doesn't. But in my opinion, it doesn't sound true.

We can do better than that.

* * *

This is the breeding ground for the devil. Trust me. Let me put it this way, God will decide which way we go. It is only by luck we are surviving. There are people who are being killed here and you find out they were torched to death. People are dying like flies.

But a community is a community. What can we do about it? It is only that the people are not committed to being a community. They are committed only to making money. They are not coming here to build anything. And whatever they find here is broken, so they are going to break it more.

Okay, this community would have worked and it might work eventually, but only if the laws are enforced. How would you feel if you have this neighbor? You are sick. You are well. It is day. It is night. This neighbor of yours doesn't worry. He just blasts away with his music. How would you feel about such a neighbor?

I mean can you imagine living in a place where there is no respect for peace and quiet, where there is commotion all hours of the day and night? No! Only in places like this do you find that.

The world is going to the dogs. Because if the people aren't heeding the laws, then only the dogs will bark and bark and do their thing. And it will be good.

Ja, and these days they will tell you about democracy and the rights of this and that. Now, this democracy is sometimes so stupid to me, because you give somebody rights in order for them to trample on other people's rights.

* * *

I am always observing the world and wondering, "Why is it this way? Is there a reason behind all of this?"

You can see we are bad, man. We are bad. And we are getting worse by the day. Like I asked you, "How is it possible for people to be good one day and then bad the next? How is that possible?"

It makes me think, "What has gotten into man to make him change overnight."

Look, I am talking about big stuff here. This is happening according to my knowledge of the world. It might take a long time for you to understand this. I am talking about is big stuff here.

When I grew up the community raised the child—the community. As I am a brother, I am a brother to her. As I am a sister, I am a sister to her. And the whole community would discipline the child.

But this has also changed. Today, if you see a child misbehaving on the street, you can't correct his behavior. If you try, the parents will come running and screaming, "Don't touch my child!" And tomorrow, when the problem is fully fleshed and they need your support, they will find that their neighbors have folded their hands. The problem has grown from the smallest seed to this monstrosity and they can't do anything about it.

Everything has changed. Today when you have a problem you stick to yourself and you might even think of killing self because you can't find help out there. But you did it to yourself, because you couldn't work with the community.

* * *

THE STORY OF THE PREACHER

There was a preacher in Jo'burg or Klerksdorp or some similar place. Now this preacher loved people. Helping here and there. Listening to their struggles, giving support, feeding the hungry, and so forth.

One day he was riding in his car and he picked up three guys hitchhiking. He stopped to give them a lift only to be killed, you know. It was like the dog biting the hand that feeds it. It was like that to me.

It made me sad when I read about it in the newspaper. I like the *Daily Sun*. It carries stories: the good, the bad, and the ugly. So I read that article and it touched me the wrong way and I felt bad.

* * *

"We all want to own things.

But who owns us? Who owns our life?

Once we understand we don't own our lives, we can live without fear."

* * *

The simple matter of it is that when the sun rises it is for all: the killers, the rapists, the whatevers, the mad, and the mad dogs and stuff. And when it rains it is always the same. It only amounts to which part of the world are you in or which part of the country are you in at that point in time. But all of these things are happening for us all and if it might not be raining for you in your part of the world that day, it will. Or it is bound to rain some other day as long as you are alive. Because when you are dead, I don't think you will be missing any rain or sunset or stuff. But if you are alive you are bound to see those things because this is part and parcel of our lives.

Generations come and generations go. But the world still remains the same. The people are waging wars, killing one another, and the very same world they are fighting for is going to swallow their blood and them personally. But at the end of the day, it just remains there.

People are always fighting and then they go ahead and make peace again. There is time for everything. Time for sewing, time for tearing things apart, time for throwing away, time for hunting stuff, time for crying, time for being happy, time for war, time for peace. It means all those things are not a mistake. They are bound to be there, because they are there.

* * *

"We have this habit of seeing
the bad things in people.

What I do know is that you can't put
a good man down."

* * *

You can get to the point where you know wrong is wrong. Look, there are some people who don't recognize their own wrongdoing. They just do it because they enjoy doing things and even if you catch them they are just big eyes. They don't understand what you mean.

Until it gets into you, this understanding of "this is wrong" or "this is right." Then you can start making decisions. It is kind of like an evaluation. I mean you have these two items. They are both heavy and you have a long walk ahead. "Can I carry both of them? Which one should I take? Which one should I leave behind?"

You get to choose what you can live with. Lately, I discovered, "No, no, this is not working out like it should. This is not the way. This is not the road." And I mean, this is not something that someone else tells you. You get to feel it. You get to live it. You get to know it. Not by being told. And you don't go to school for that one. It just comes natural. You don't go to school for that one.

I just pray to God that one day the people will see the light at the end of the tunnel like I do. Because nobody showed me, I just saw it. So maybe they will too. But if they don't that's not my problem. But I will always be praying for them, "Lord, God, please try to make these people of Woodlane Village and me included see the light at the end of the tunnel."

* * *

QUOTE ABOVE DONALD'S BED

"It is not the critic who counts; not the man who points out how the strong man stumbles, or where the doer of deeds could have done them better. The credit belongs to the man who is actually in the arena, whose face is marred by dust and sweat and blood;

who strives valiantly; who errs, who comes short again and again, because there is no effort without error and shortcoming; but who does actually strive to do the deeds; who knows great enthusiasms, the great devotions; who spends himself in a worthy cause; who at the best knows in the end the triumph of high achievement, and who at the worst, if he fails, at least fails while daring greatly, so that his place shall never be with those cold and timid souls who neither know victory nor defeat." —Theodore Roosevelt

* * *

"This is South Africa. Nothing comes easy. And nothing comes cheap."

* * *

My worry again is some people are accumulating wealth as best they could. Thousands, millions and millions in order for them to just die and leave those stuff out there for people who didn't even sweat for it. They just don't say enough is enough. So what does that tell you?

Look, this is not a thing of black or white. This is a thing of you being a human being and respecting peoples' rights or something.

You know I have this old man, you know this Mandela old guy. He seemed stupid to some people because they said after taking over as president he should have said, "Kill the whites!" No! Look, in this nation . . . not one race can live without the other. We are here to be together. No one can live without the other. So if you think you can live without another, you are wrong.

Look let's use the example of Zimbabwe. They just tried to chase the whites away. Are they faring better? No! They are worse than they did the first time. Because, look, you take a plot from the white man but you can't manage it. Now where you going? What are you doing?

Look these people are taking plots that they can't manage. They take a plot that is thriving. It has everything. They take it after one year that plot goes down, down, until it is rubble instead of it being a plot or a mielie field or whatever. You don't do that. If you do that you kill self. I mean I never went to school, but my common sense tells me that if these people tried to combine, to work together they would have done better.

* * *

You see, I don't have a friend. Acquaintances I have many . . . they just say "Hey!" They are passing by but they can't come in. Because we are beyond that coming in and being together. Because you just have to be yourself in order to be with somebody for a couple of minutes, a couple of hours. Because if you rob me once, you can rob me twice. You rob me once you say, "Sorry." I don't expect it twice. You do it twice I know you are not sorry, you just are what you are. Now, I can't say that I won't greet you. "Hey, how's that, Don?" "Hey, hi! Good." But you are passing. You are not getting in like you did the first time.

* * *

We are living with people. Don't take people for granted. Remember, one thing: "have the friends that you can like to have on your side." Instead of just having any friend who might just sell you out for fifty cents. Don't go for that. Have a friend that you can even die for. I mean I am trying to impress on you to think about this friendship thing. We don't have to take anybody for a friend.

I don't have a friend other than Happy and you, Pieter. Because I know what friends can do. You can have a friend and a friend can hurt you more than you can hurt for your whole life. That's why I don't need a friend. But those I have, especially like Happy and you, I mean, if I am hurting by you, I can handle it but not anybody else. Because I can kill him, I can even strangle him. Just get hold of his neck until he dies. Now I don't need that. I don't need that at all.

* * *

DIALOGUE BETWEEN DONALD AND ME

Donald: "I realize in life every question has an answer by itself. Not you, worrying self. But stuff solves self."

Me: "There is a saying, 'Every problem carries the seeds of its own solution.' Every question contains an answer."

Donald: "Every action has a reaction."

Me: "But in order to get to some of the answers in life, you have to enter a space of uncertainty and that space calls into question everything you once knew."

Donald: "Yebo."

Me: "And you have to be fearless enough to face ambiguity. You have to go to places that make your head hurt. But only when you do that...."

Donald: "... will you know whether it works or it doesn't. It goes on and on. It doesn't stop. It goes on until you get it right. And you can't fail. You are meant to win. But only by understanding and exploring what we are talking about. But we are afraid of the unknown. That's why I say human beings are creatures of habit. They need their habitat."

Me: "But that is what you and I have experienced in our own way. We ventured into the unknown together."

Donald: "You can say that again!"

Me: "It was the unknown of becoming friends."

Donald: "And now again, when I am telling people about you they don't believe. They think there is magic working here. I am not worried about that. Because remember, I didn't plan it. I don't know how it came about. But when it happened I didn't doubt it. I just grabbed hold. And you didn't doubt it. You just went."

Me: "Yes, we took a leap of faith."

Donald: It is misunderstood by many people. Even me, sometimes I don't understand it, but I just try to get to know it. And work towards bettering it. I told you, Pieter, it is impossible. Remember, when we went to Tembisa I was talking to Chris about writing a book and me not being able to do so. Maybe, I can buy a tape recorder and speak my whole life's story.... But that's a tall order. You know what I am talking about? And all of a sudden here comes, Pieter. Now, what do you think about that?"

Me: "I know. It is hard to explain."

Donald: "I can't even account for it. But this is life! This is what I love about life, Pieter."

Me: "I never imagined that I would be part of building stories with you. Because I lived with you and we had adventures together that generated new stories."

Donald: "Exactly! That is something else again. This is what seems amazing to me now. This is something really new. This is new page in my life. It is unplanned. It is only that it is what it is."

Me: "Donald, I hope you realize it is mutual."

Donald: "Let me put it this way...this experience has taught me humility. Pieter, I am this guy who can get really angry. And angry to hurt—fast, quick—and then get sorry later. But after I met you, I have learned something. You are not teaching me by saying, 'don't do this or that,' but by being you. You are somebody who listens."

* * *

Pieter, you have to live it before you can write about it.

If you want to know what it's like to stay in a shack then you have to stay in a shack.

But you did it!

It's the real thing.

* * *

THE STORY OF THE SUFFERING GUY

So there is the story of this suffering guy. He has this old *bakkie* with odd-colored doors. You know, the doors are from different vehicles. And one wheel of the bakkie is bigger than the others. And when it rides, it goes bumping, bumping along—like a cripple hobbling on a stiff leg.

Now this guy is going about his own business, trying to make ends meet. And there are these other guys who drive this BMW. It is stolen and they are on a getaway with a bag full of cash. Let's say R3 million. The police are chasing them so they think, "We are going to be caught. We must stash the money." They take the bag and toss it in the back of the poor guy's truck. And he doesn't even notice, because the vehicle is always making funny noises.

And when he gets home, he goes to bed. He is tired and miserable. In the morning, he wakes up and looks at his dirty truck and says, "No, man. This old bakkie of mine needs a wash. I must give it a shine." And then, "Hey, what is this bag in here? And upon opening it, "Oh my God! Whoa, whoa!"

Now look, this guy didn't plan on getting money. He was suffering. But suddenly he is a wealthy man. I mean a multimillionaire, a couple of millions rich. He didn't earn the money. He was merely at the right place at the right time.

This is how things happen in life. It is about "timing." Everything has its time. You can't change it. You have to accept it. Everything happens for a reason. Knowing the reason beforehand can help, but afterwards it is a matter of time. It makes no sense to worry about what has come to pass. Can we turn back the hands of time?

* * *

"Your comfort is somebody else's discomfort."

* * *

CONVERSATIONS ON THE RIDE HOME

1.

I don't know if you know, but there are times when I am sitting alone. It is night. I am trying to read a book because I am always a reader. After reading I just close the book and then I feel tears running down my face . . . tears, hot. I am not crying for anything in particular. But there is something that ails me, that doesn't sit well. Now, I was not aiming on it and I was not thinking about it. And there are stuff that I should cry about, I don't cry. I just look and I do what I get to do. But from nowhere when there is nothing happening, there comes these tears. And you find out I'm just crying for a couple of what-ever. Can you explain that? What does that mean anyway, Pieter? Am I normal or am I *sickenyana*?

2.

My worry is just living better and just being able to take care of self and family. And that's all I ask for. Not much, not less. Because if it's less, it means I am in the "suffering line." But if it is just in the level where I can survive on a day-by-day basis and when somebody dies I just get to bury them and then heal as best I can. Then I am good.

3.

I can't claim to be good, Pieter. No. I can't claim to be a good guy. But one thing that I know is that I am getting to accept me for who I am and again I am not into this ... you know, as people, all of us want to be a winner. But now, I am not playing for a win. I am just playing for survival. And you know, by survival I am talking about me not sleeping with a hungry stomach.

4.

I mean it is a struggle to go where I want to. But I am in a better position than others. There are people that are worse out there. So if I am trying to cry, I am just mocking those guys out there who are really in the suffering line. Because me personally, I might be in the line of helping them out. We get to do what we get to do in order to make the world a better place to live for others.

But then you shouldn't have to worry about others while you are suffering. You should worry about self. Like you see in this community. Here it is, *God for us all, every man for himself.*

5.

We think about now and not tomorrow. And then we don't worry about the future because we think it will take of itself. But most of the time the future will not take care of itself. It is us who take care of the future.

We are selfish, we want to live for self and take all the credit for self. Not giving to others. That's where we fail. Now sometimes when all the favors come to you, you should just say, "Whoa, whoa, whoa," and give it to somebody else. Then you are doing something.

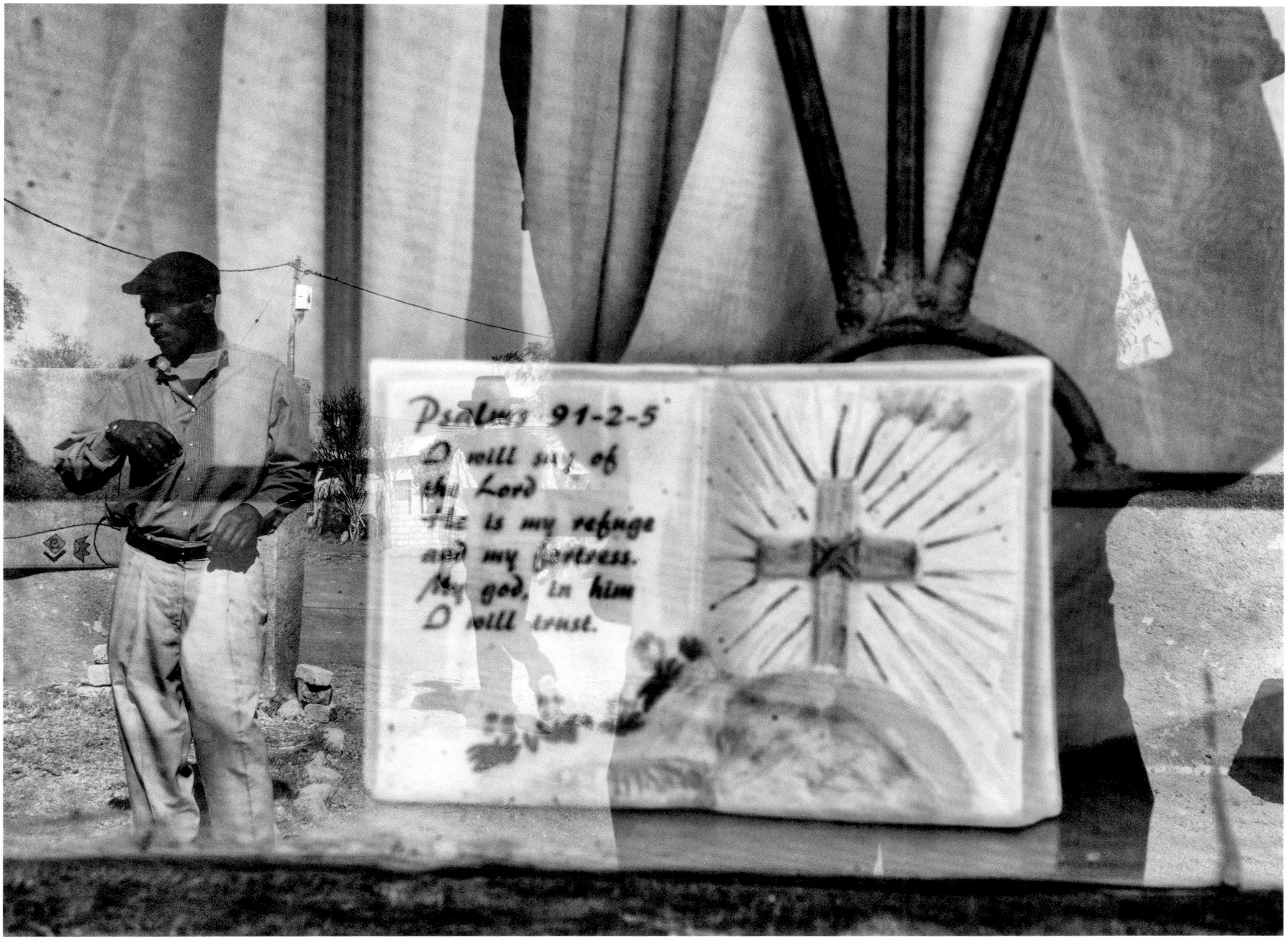

Reflection of Donald in the window of his mother's home in Soshanguve (August 2015)

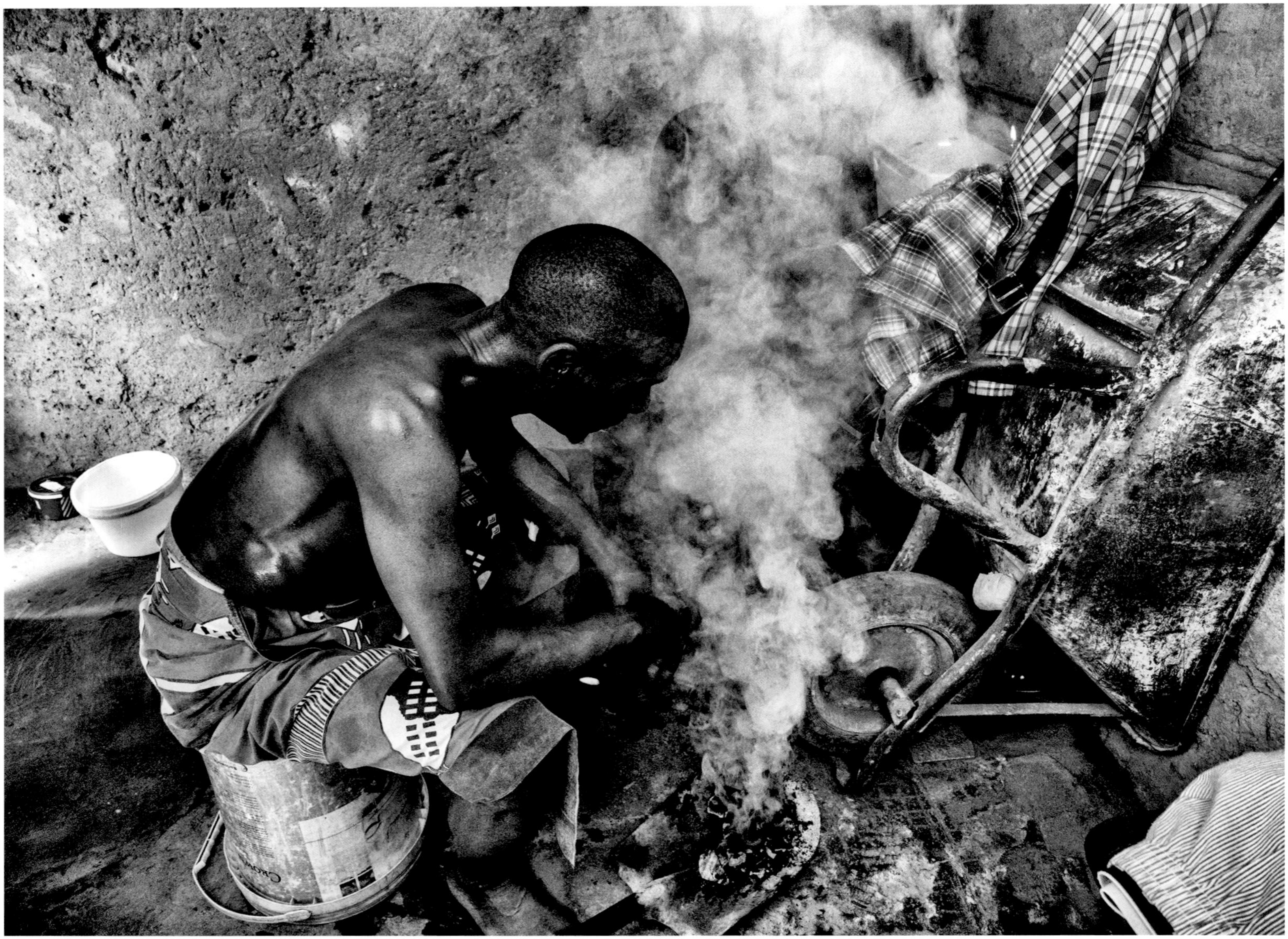

Donald cleanses in a ceremony organized by his son, Wonder (September 2017)

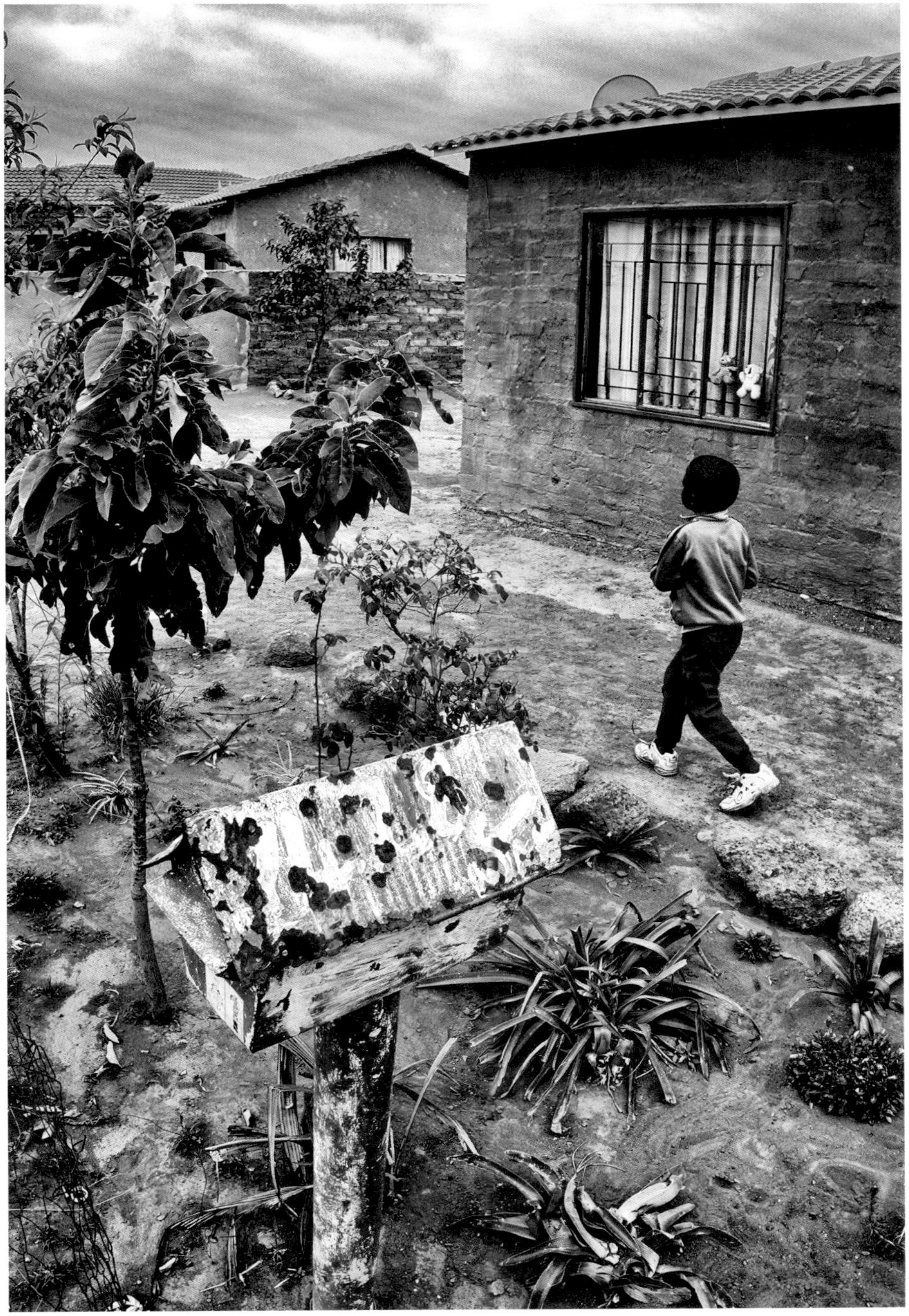

The home of Donald's son, Wonder, in Mamelodi (September 2012)

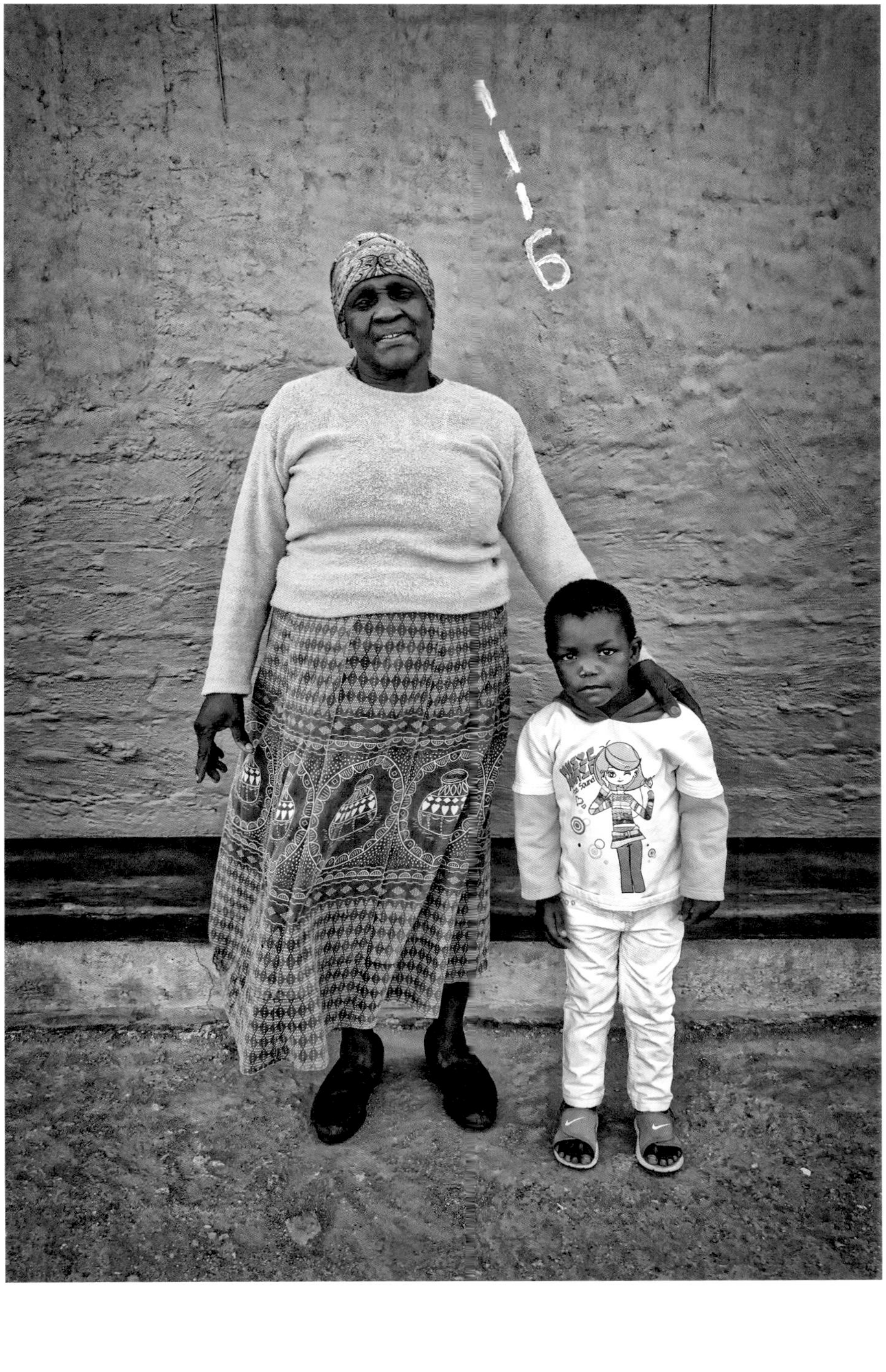

Annah with grandchild
(September 2012)

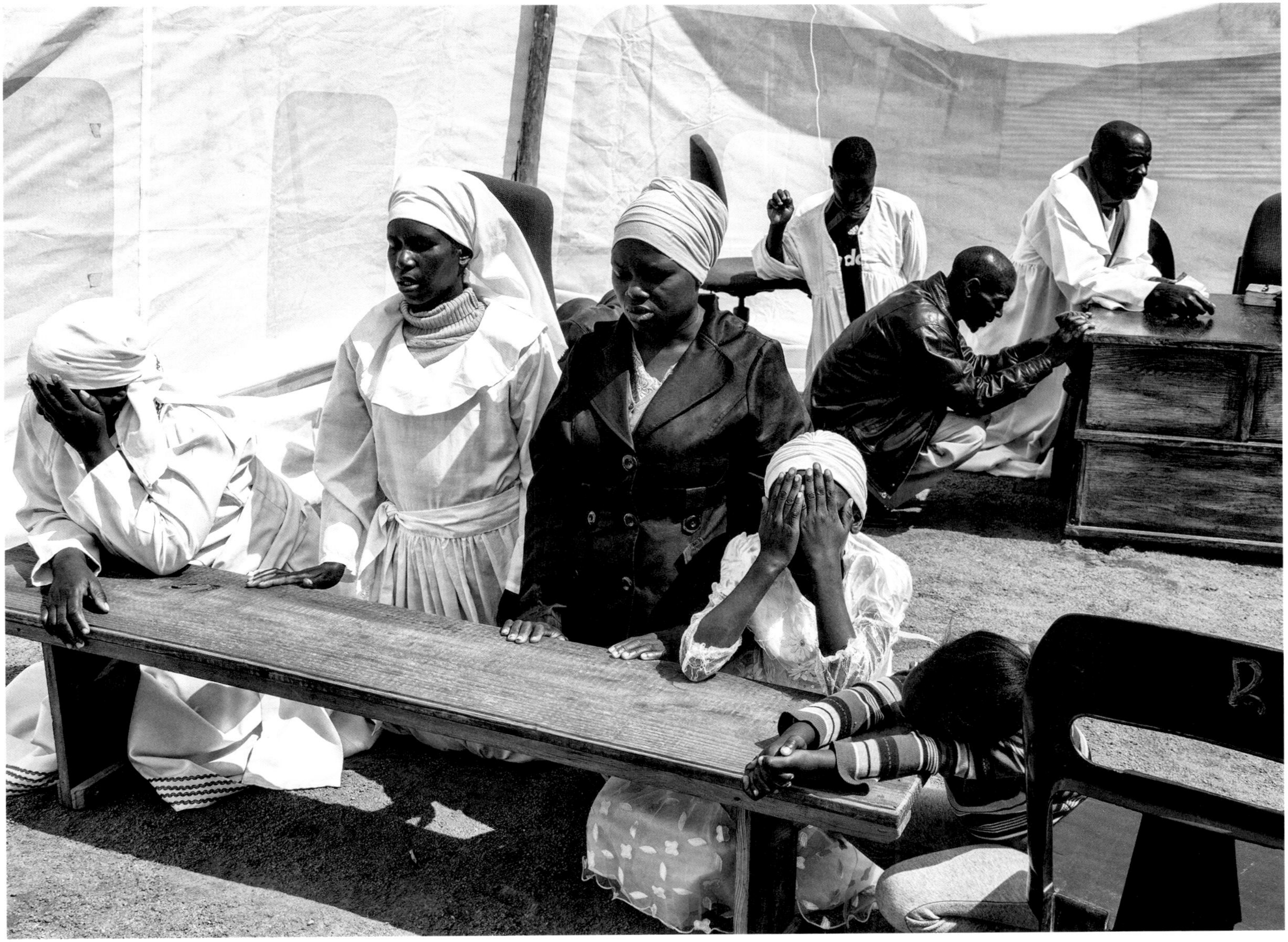

"We walk by faith, not by sight" —Donald (August 2017)

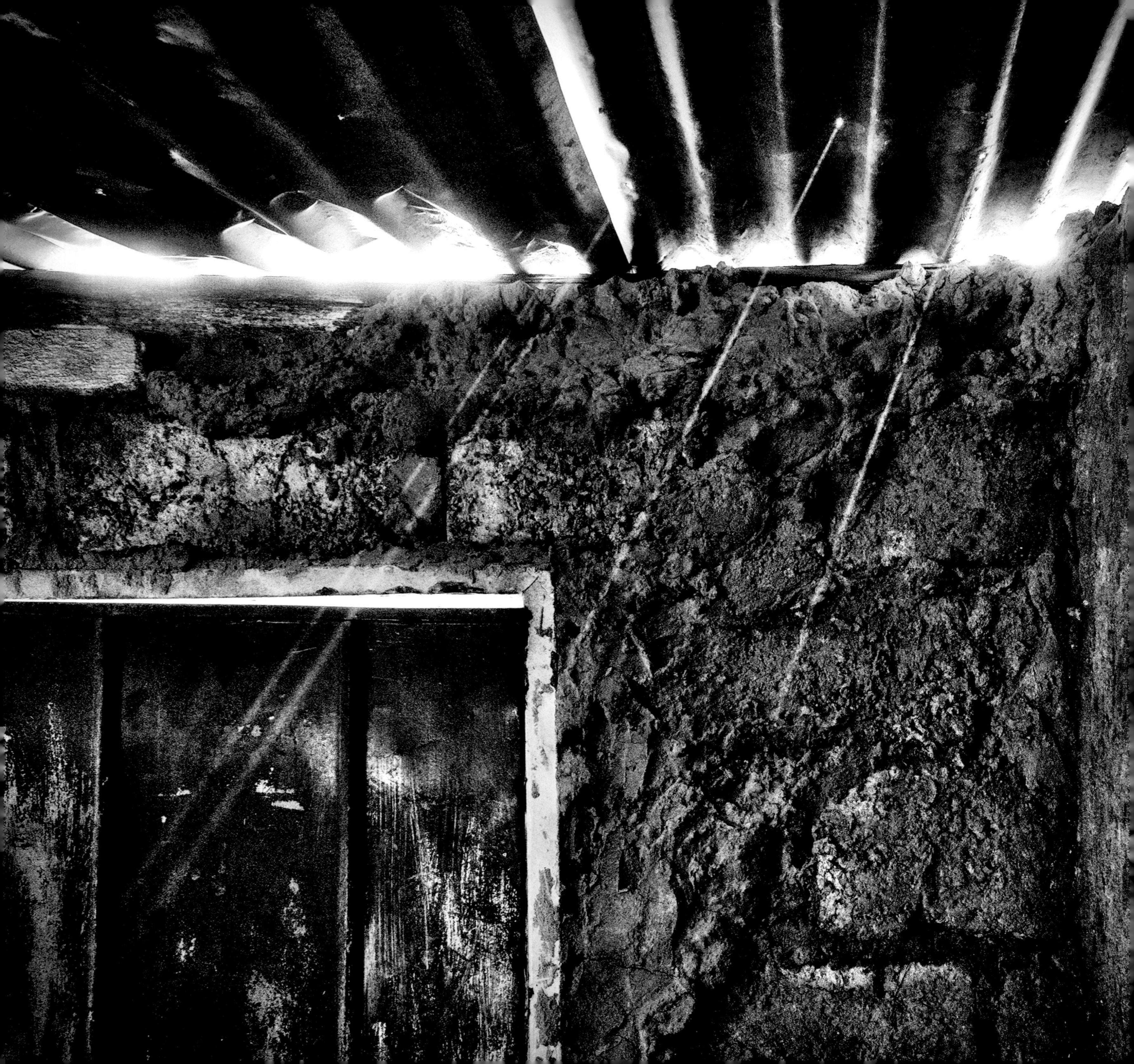

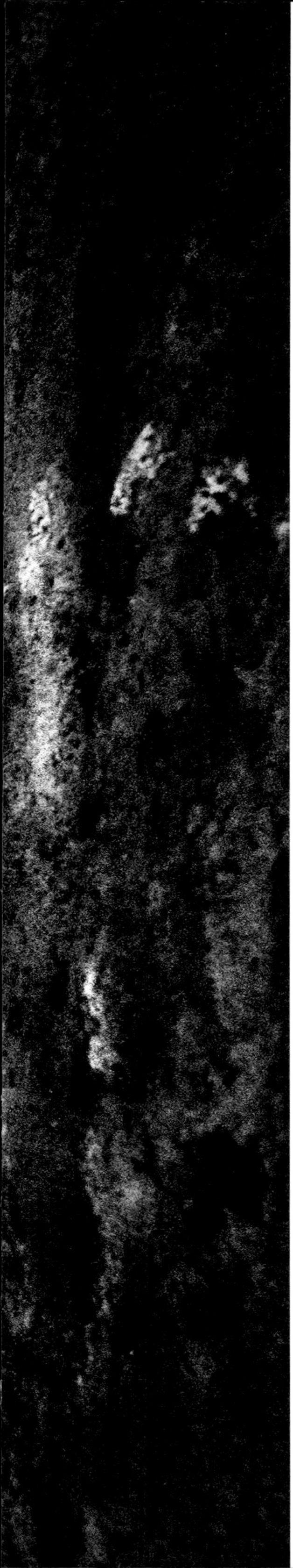

Beams of light #1
(September 2017)

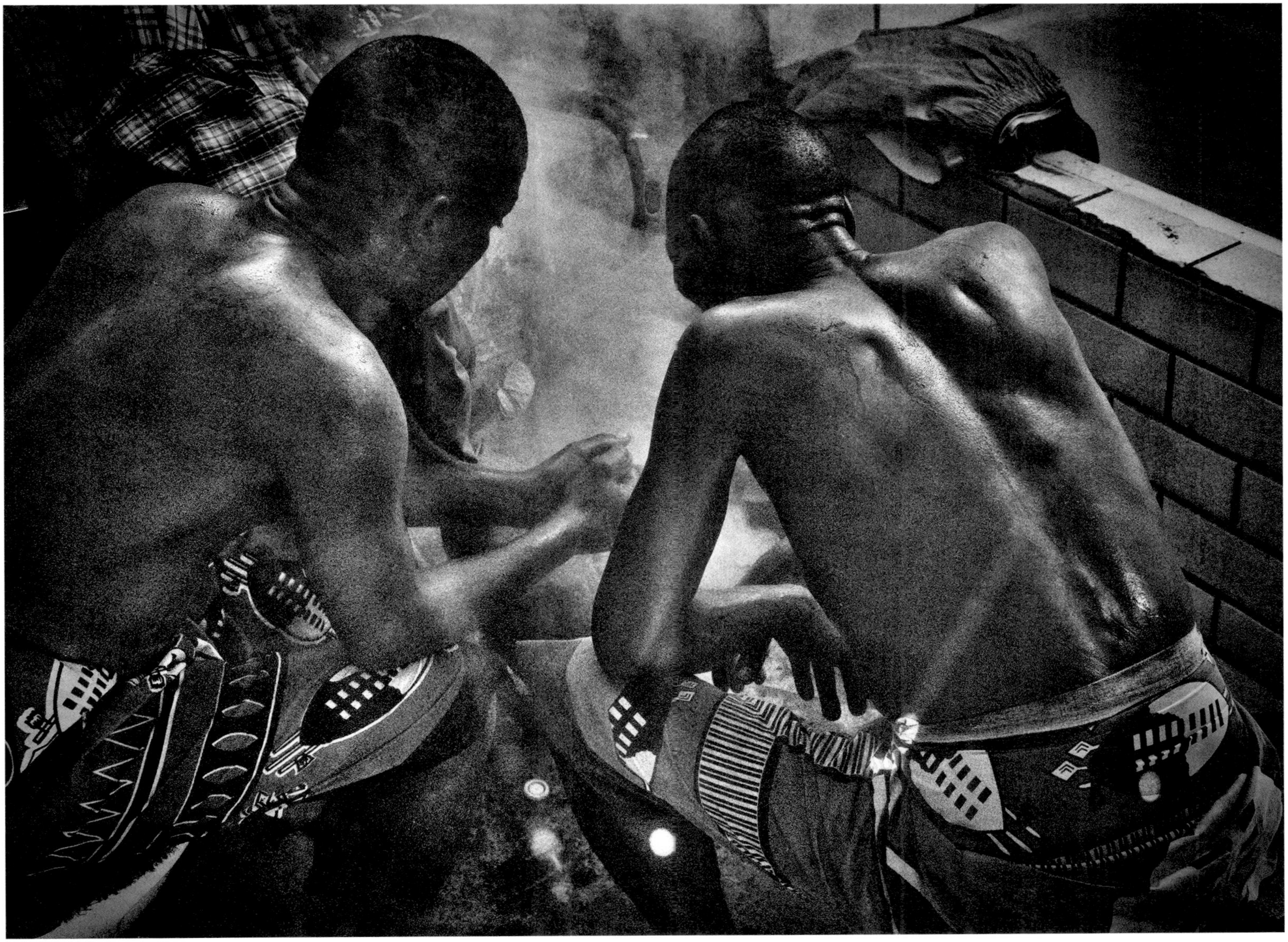

Beams of light #2 (September 2017)

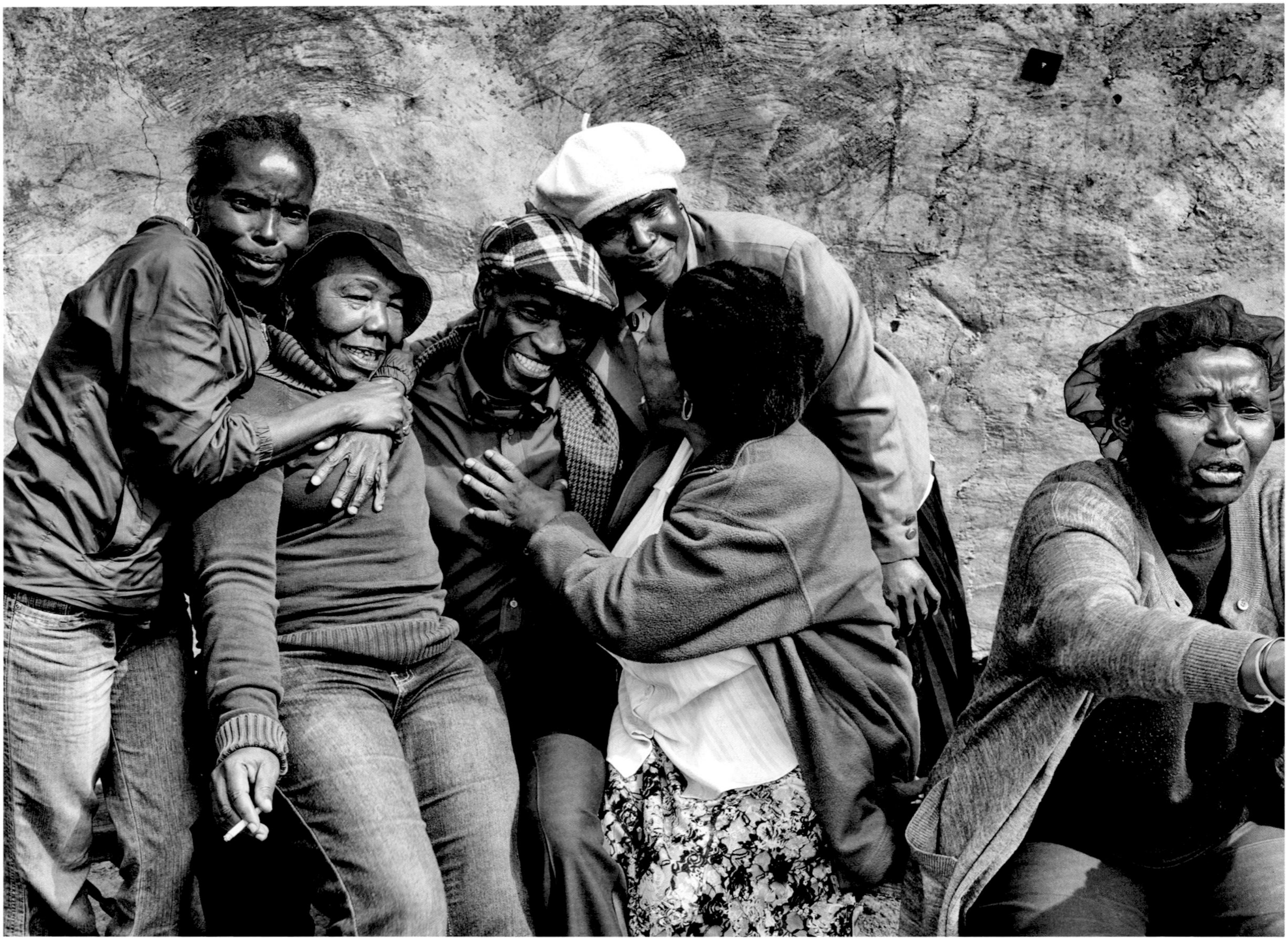

Donald reunites with his family in Winterveld, Gauteng (September 2012)

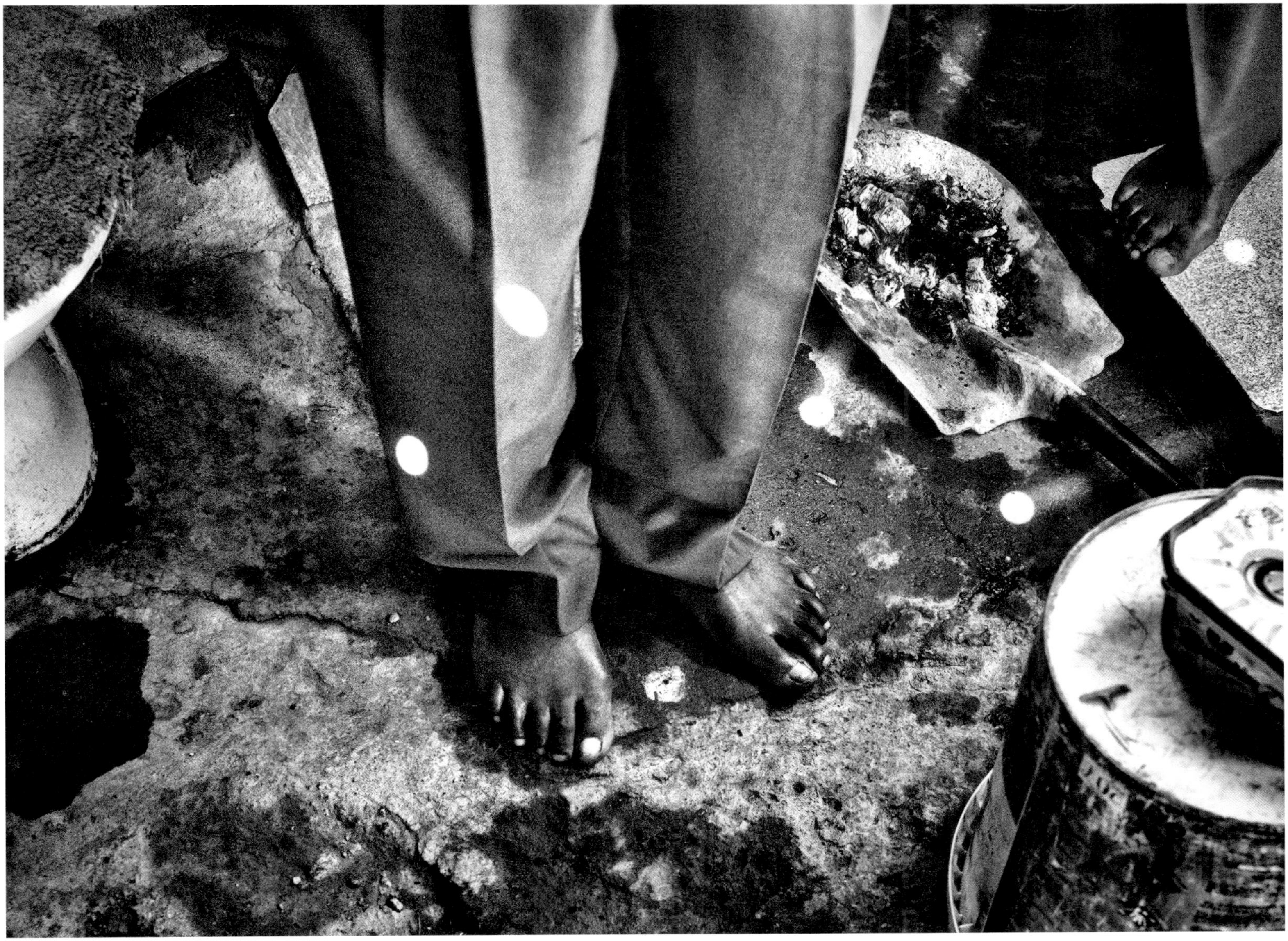

Beams of light #3 (September 2017)

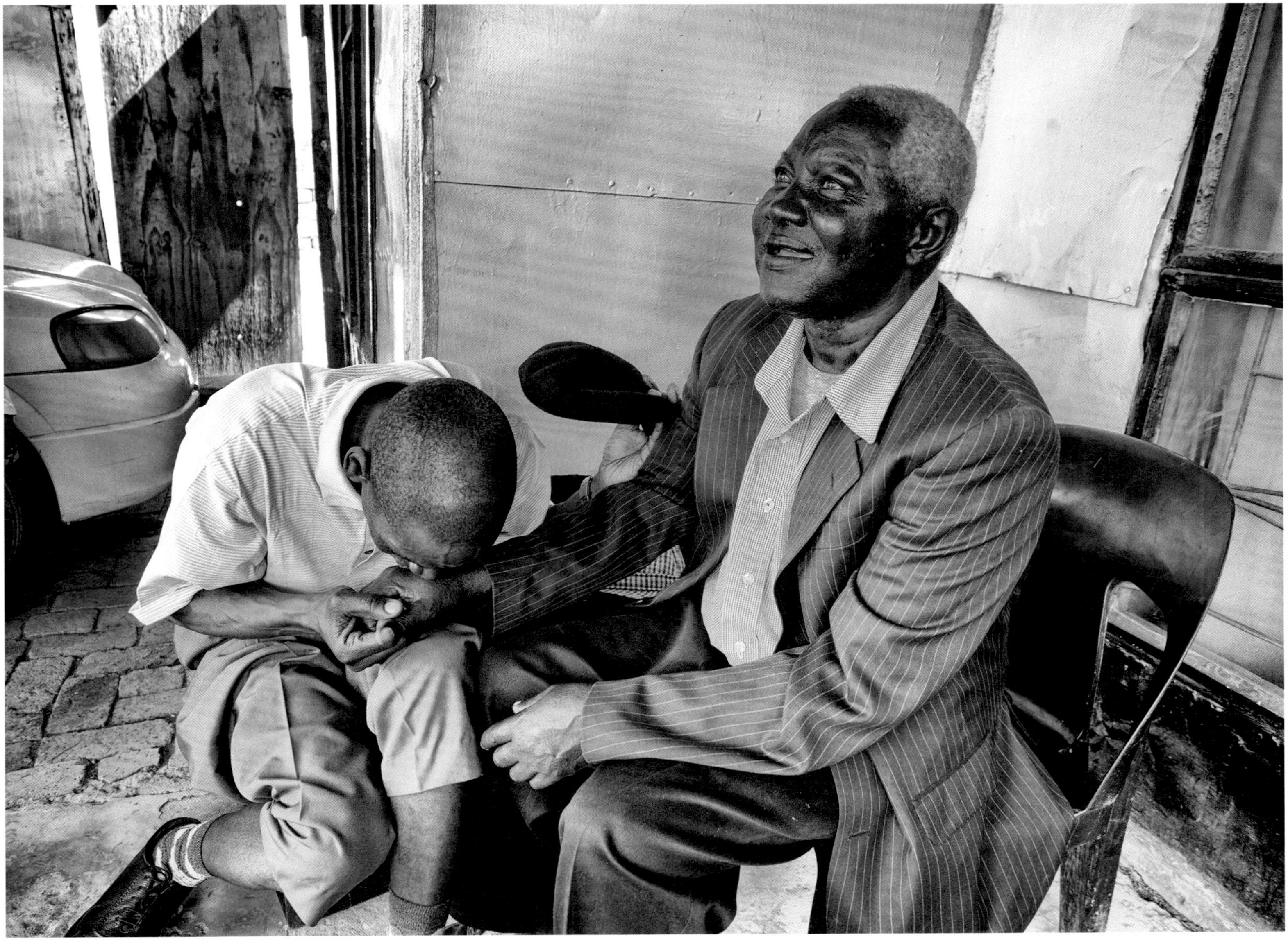

Donald pays respect (August 2015)

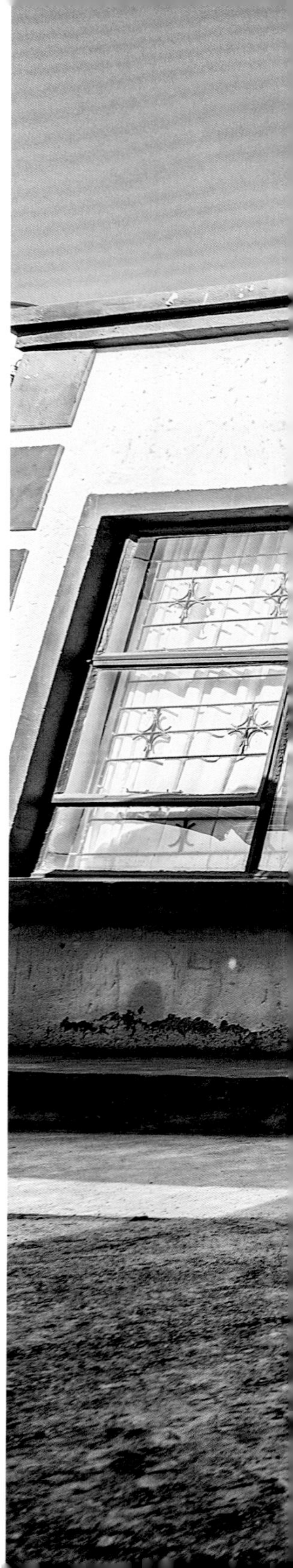

Donald dances at a family gathering in Soshanguve (August 2016)

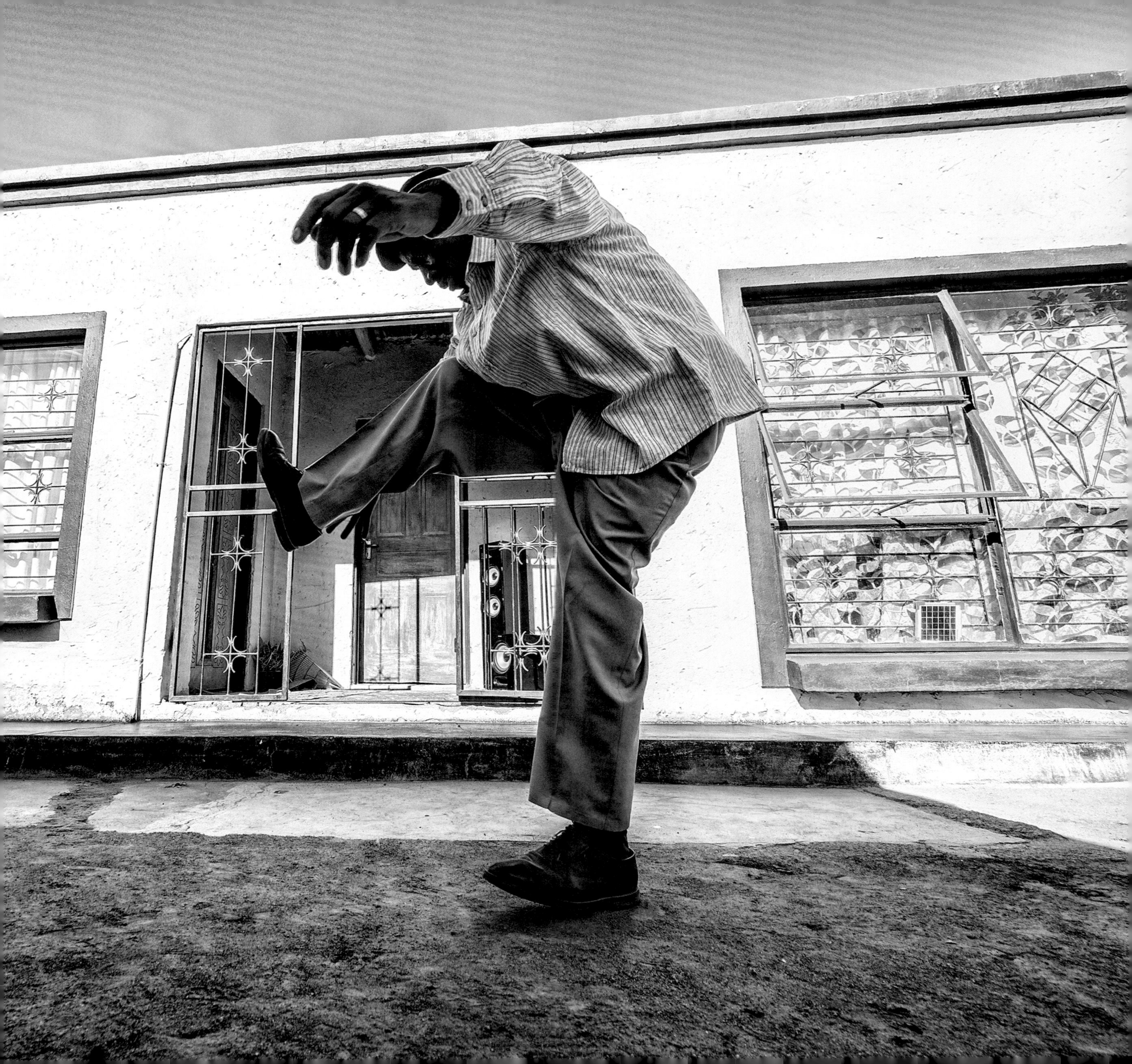

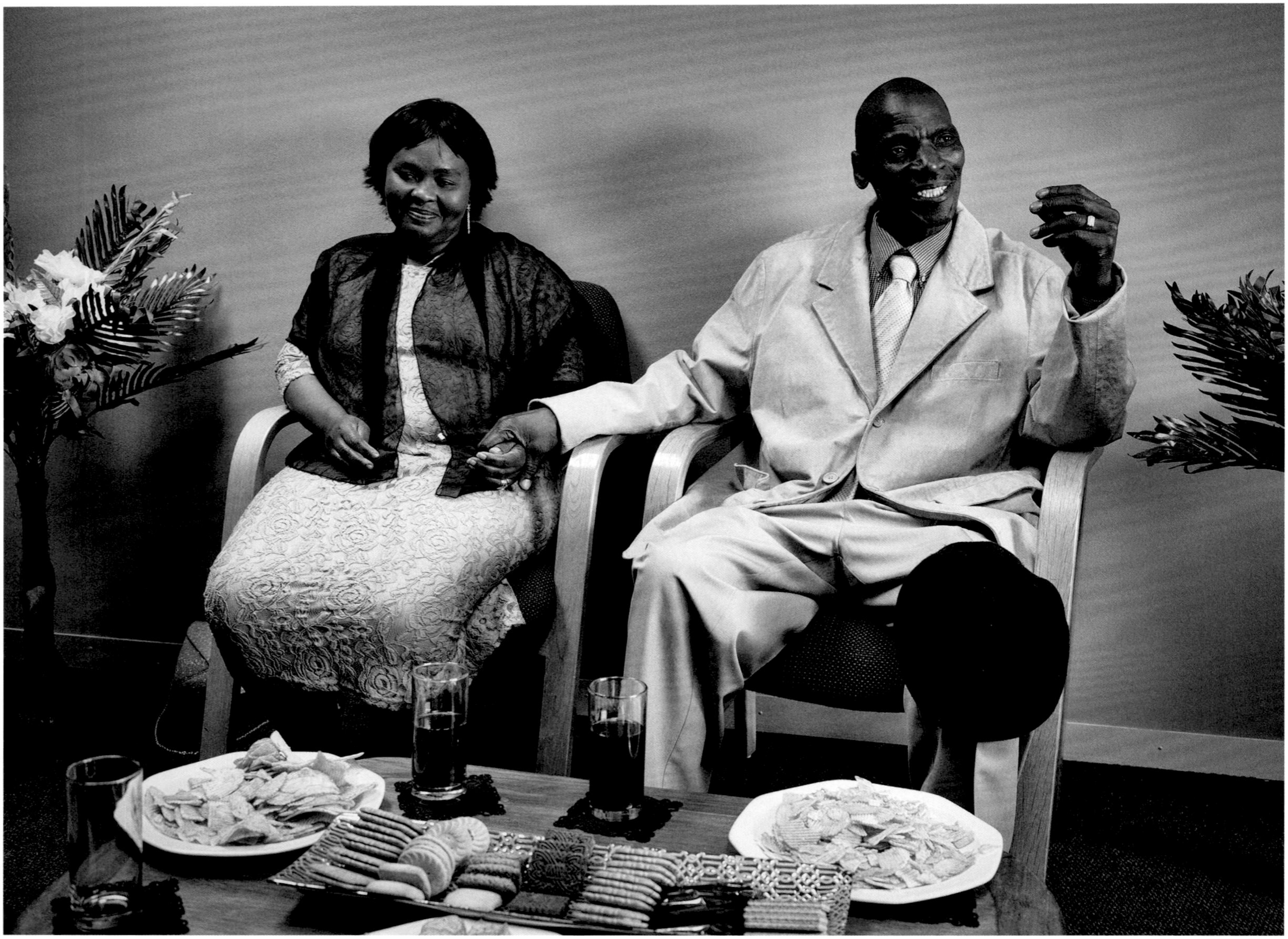

Donald and Rose at their wedding (August 2015)

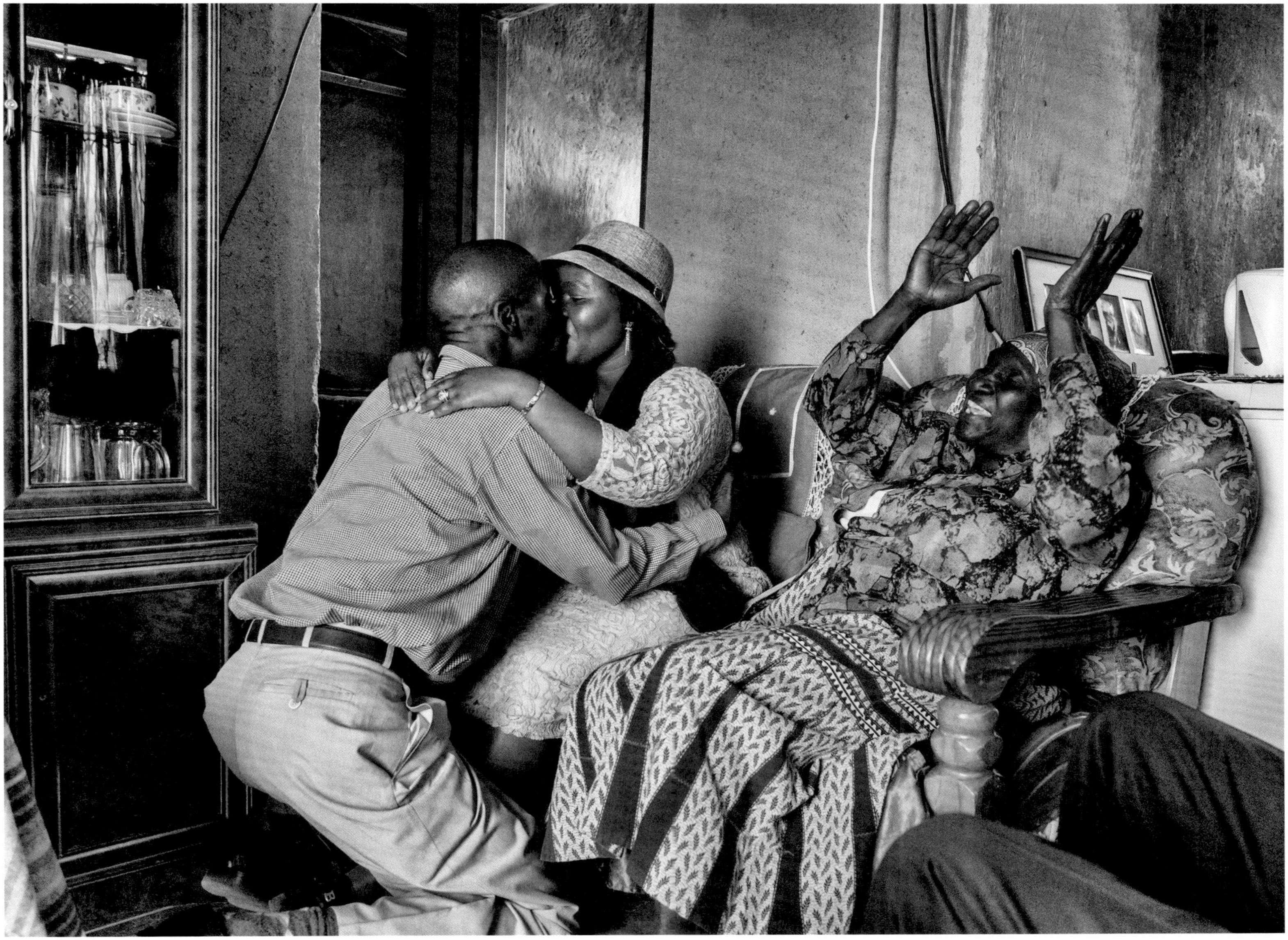

Husband and wife (August 2015)

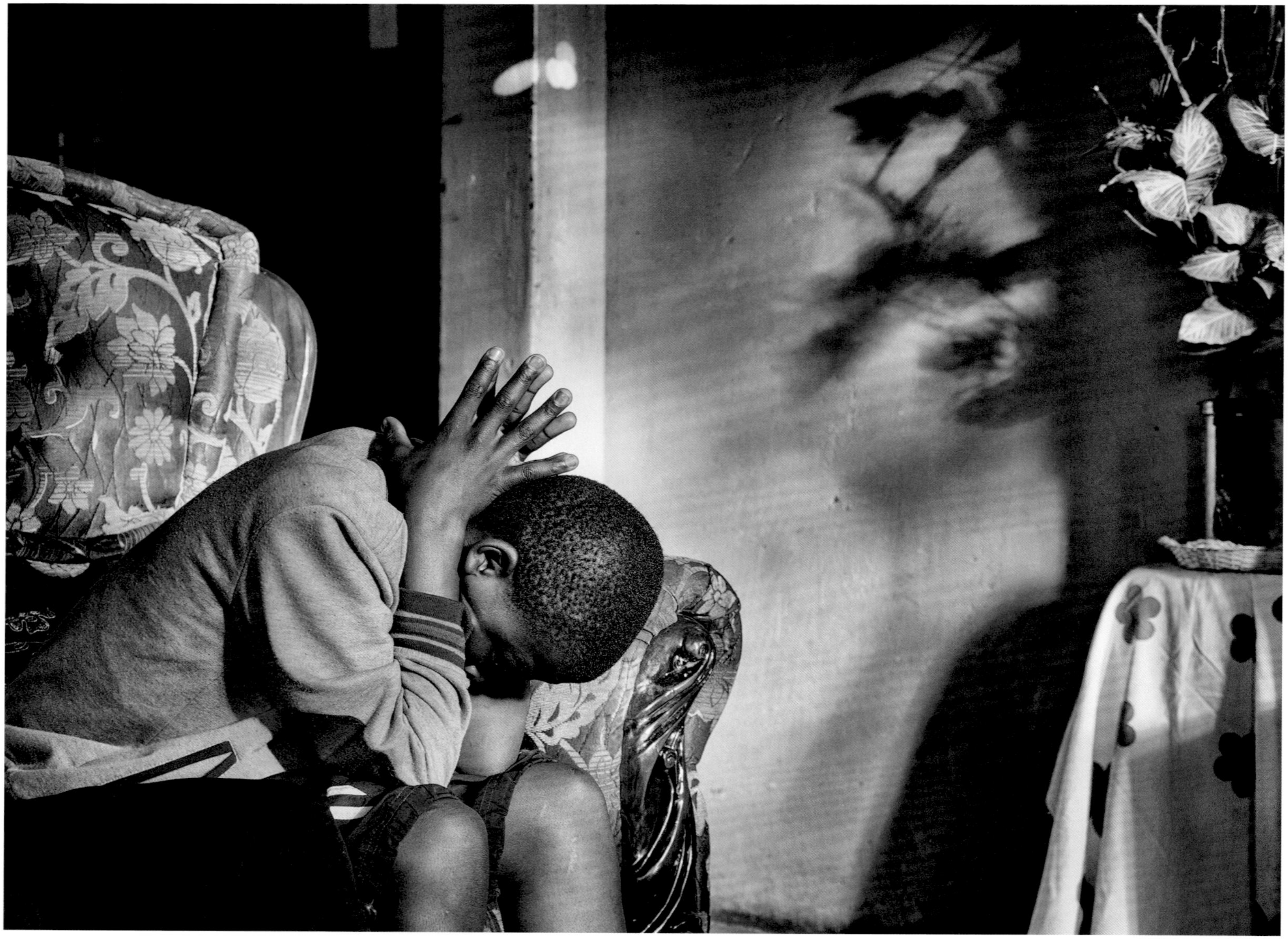

Wonder, Donald's son and traditional healer in training (August 2015)

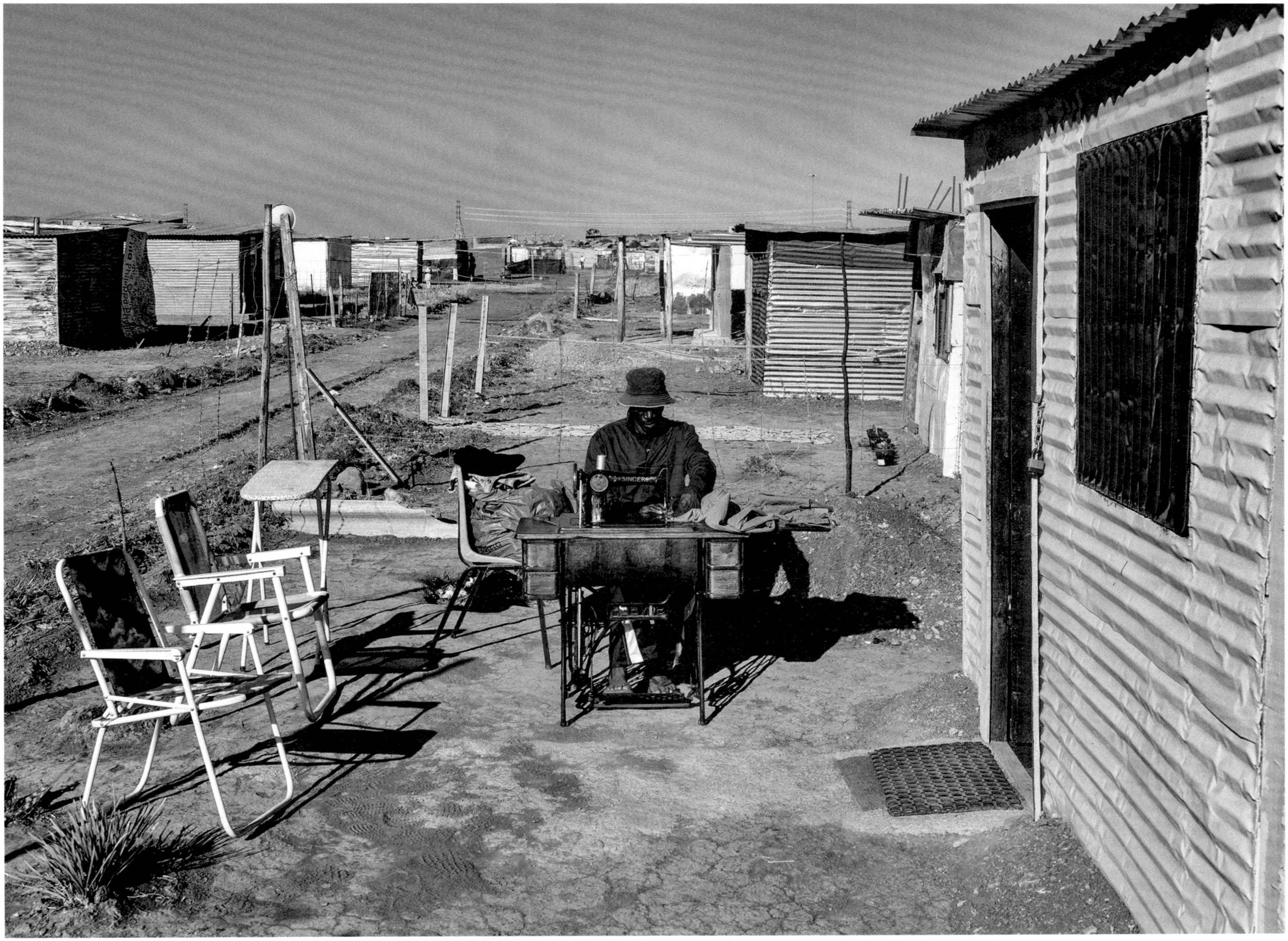

Donald at his new stand in Solomon Mahlangu Village, an informal settlement near the township of Mamelodi (August 2018). In the pursuit of a place called home, he relocated to this community in late 2017. The future of this settlement is uncertain with rumors of impending forced removals.

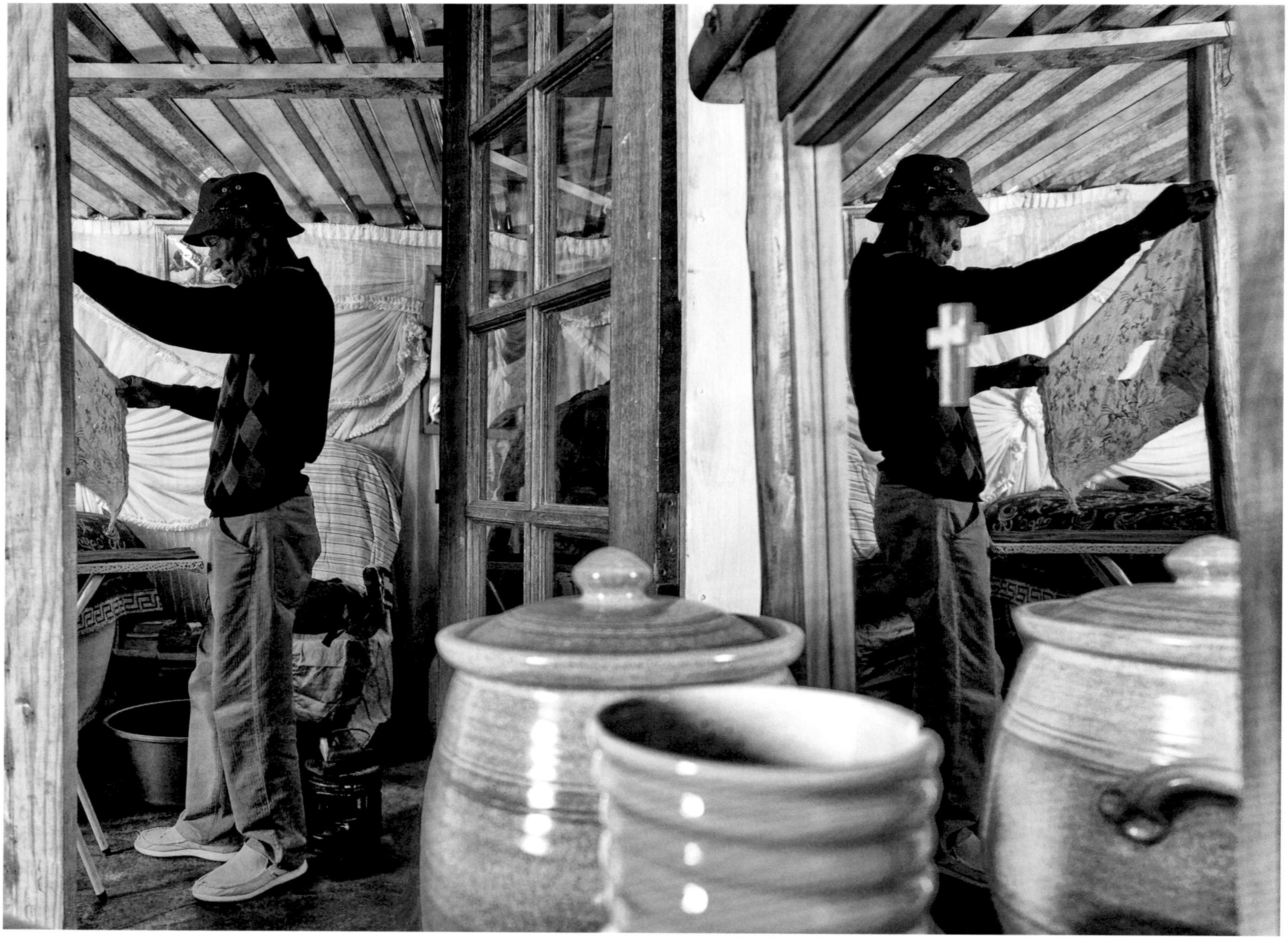

Sunday chores in Solomon Mahlangu Village (August 2018)

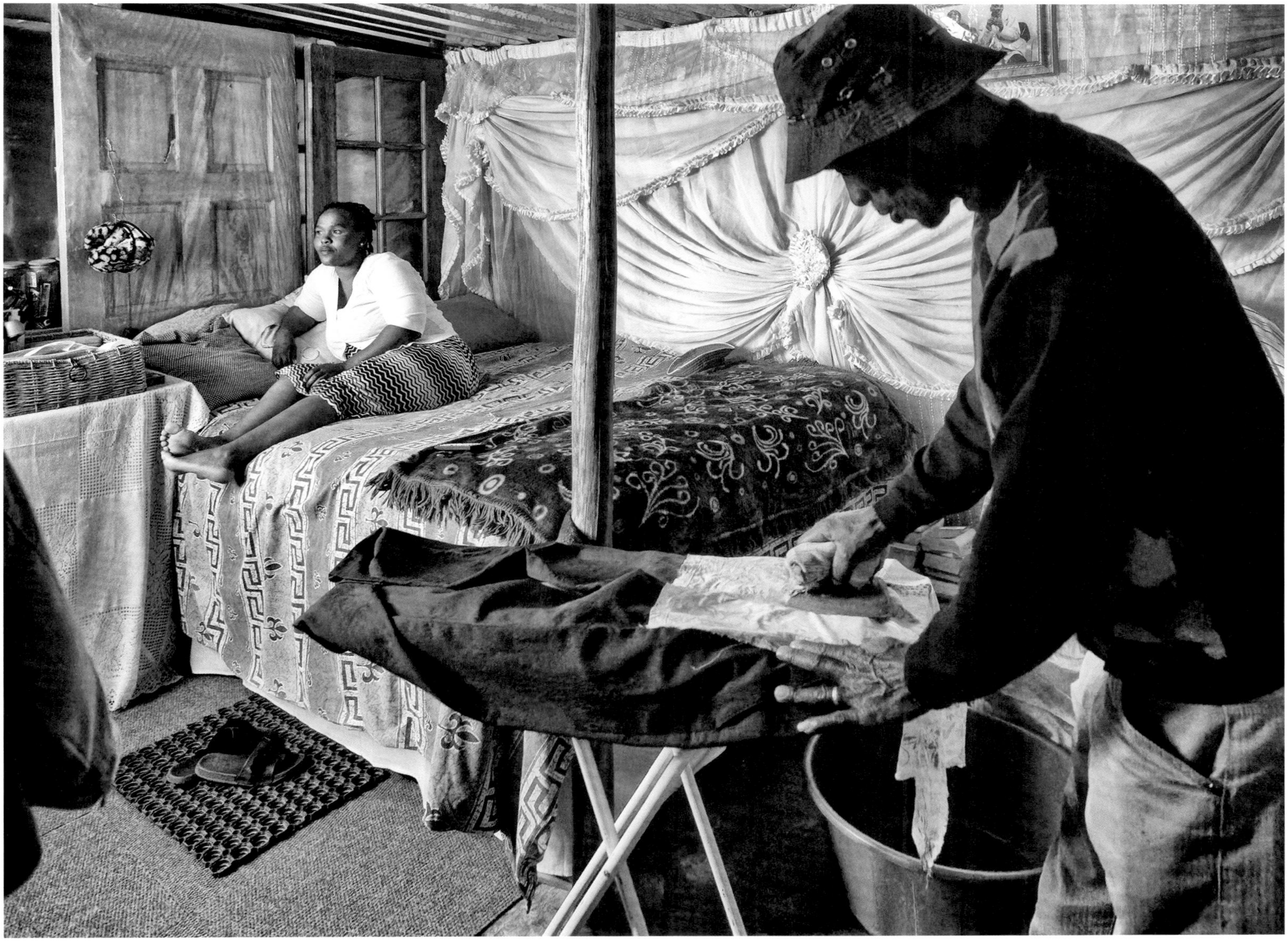

Donald irons his trousers in the shack he shares with Rose in Solomon Mahlangu Village (August 2018)

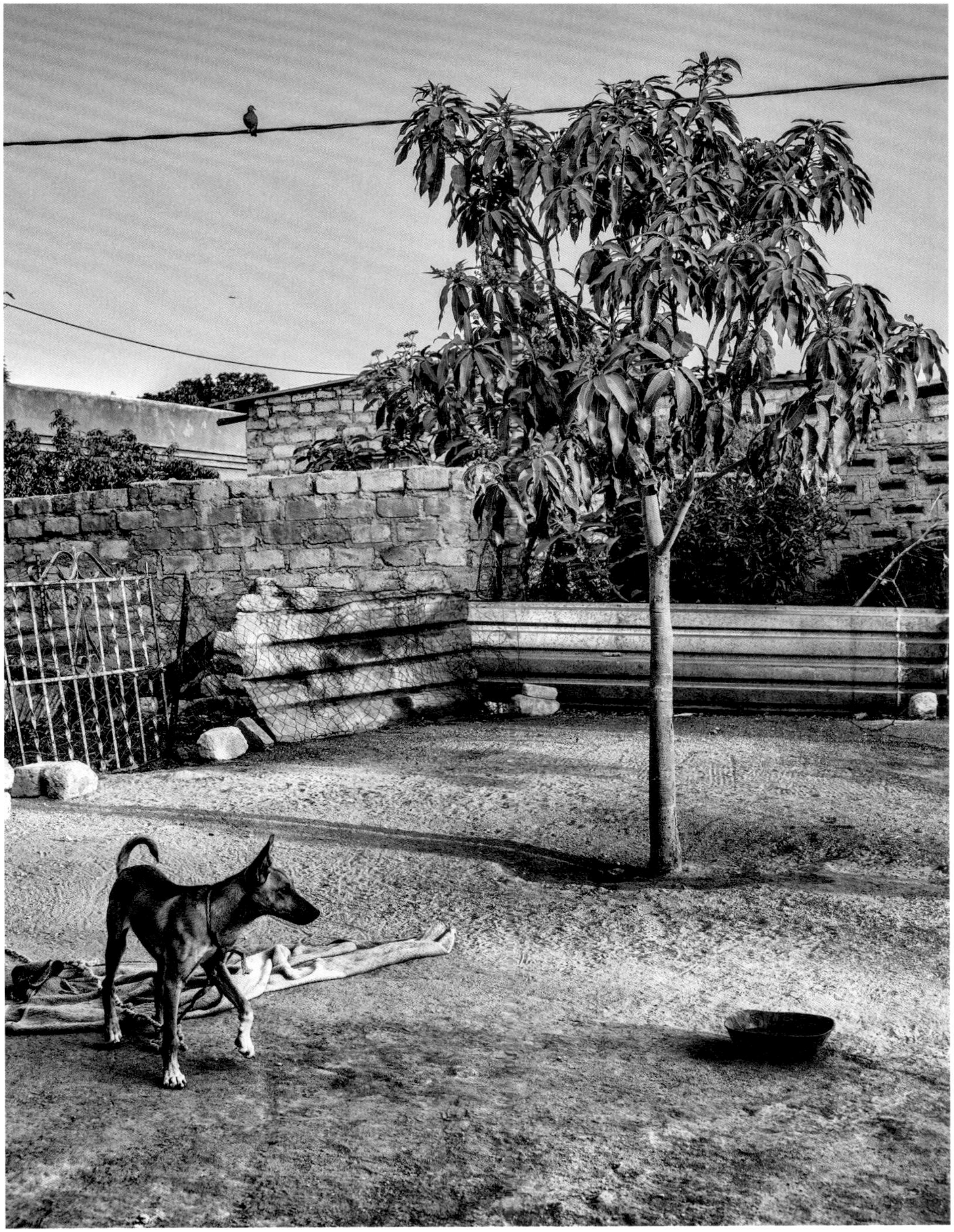

Evening at the home of Donald's in-laws in KwaMhlanga (September 2017)

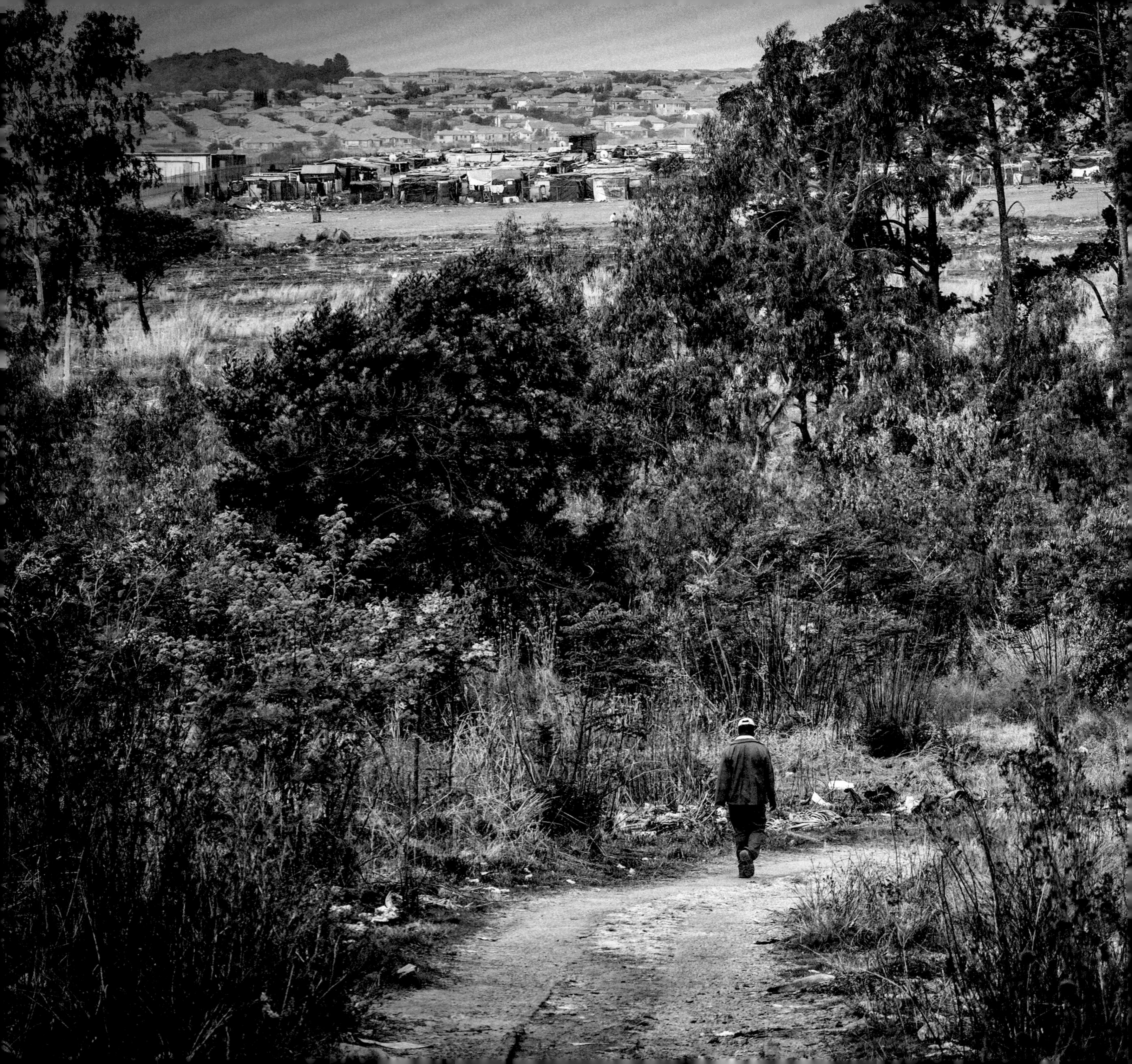

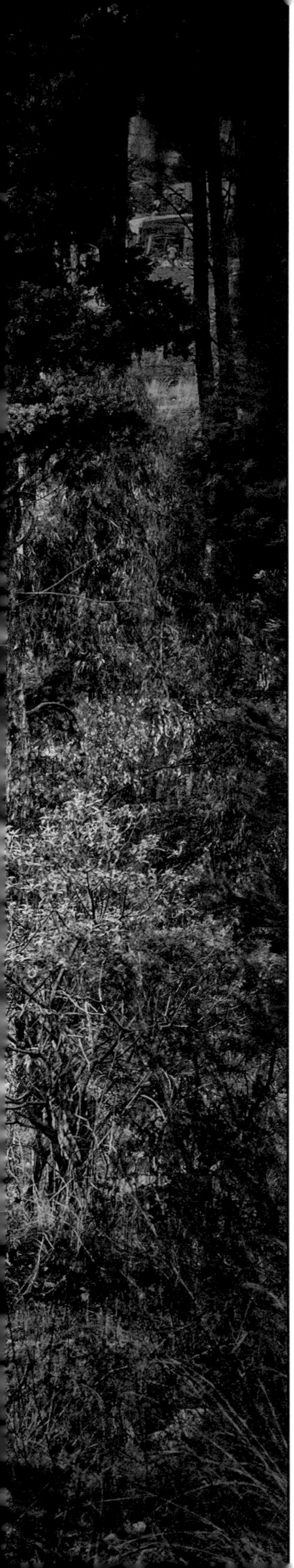

One of the many trails
leading to Woodlane Village
(September 2017)

THE LOCALE OF THE SACRED

—Stephan de Beer

Spatiality is everything. It is where we are born and die. Where we raise our children and cry. It is where we play or pray or love or fight. Where we dwell and make life and love and dreams come true. It is where we are lost. Or find our way. It is where we have our roots. Or are not allowed to root. It is where we are too far away to share the table of abundance. Or so close to the abundance that we deem ourselves fit to determine who may be seated and who not. Spatiality has to do with that intimate space of personhood, dignity, and soul. But also with that violent space of intimate betrayal. It carries dreams and resembles vengeance. It hurts and heals. Spaces are never neutral. But made. Distorted. Beautified.

The images in this collection are hauntingly beautiful. Their beauty lies in the raw and honest capture of everyday living in an urban informal settlement. Far from romanticizing struggle or poverty, this collection does the opposite: it is a provocative declaration of life over death; hope over despair; tenacity over hardship.

It shows the resistance of a people who are denied access to the city. It is a resistance, expressed not in violence or in sophisticated forms of protest, but in the resilience of people simply living their lives. They put down their roots, work out the mundane—sometimes exciting—details of living in an informal settlement, and are tenacious in their resolve to remain in this space. Their lives, as told through the images, convey something of the sacred to be found in the ordinariness of life. Woodlane Village, through the lenses of this collection, is, to me, "God taking place."

Bergmann (2008:70–97), in speaking of "God taking place," refers to the moment, or process, of valuing "the local and the spatial as an epiphany of the divine, as a sacred space in which, through creative activity and the words of dwelling, humanity can experience something of the transcendent" (Graham & Lowe, 2009:49). Some of the images in this collection depict the sacred as expressed in worship or religious ritual. But, even more poignantly, the sacred gains expression in images of friendship, children at play, homecoming, communality, and embrace.

Whilst the big church seating 7,000 people sometimes provides the background décor to the stage of life which is Woodlane Village, the images captured here subvert the notion of the sacred as restricted only to religious spaces, boldly asserting "a sacralisation of the physical, the spatial—and . . . the environmental—as an arena for redemption" (Graham & Lowe, 2009:49). The informal settlement becomes the locale of the sacred, in the same way that redemption is not far away for the big church overlooking it.

In making their lives and places on a daily basis, the residents of Woodlane Village not only create a community where a few years ago there was nothing, but also forces open, through their lives and presence in this place, opportunities and multiple invitations for redemption: socio-spatial relationships between people from different economic or racial groups; public land for the public good; churches for the work of socio-spatial justice; the landless poor to land; and the urban poor to practice agency in processes of city-making.

THE ILLUSION OF A (POST)APARTHEID CITY

Today in South Africa we live the illusion of a (post)apartheid city. Although much has changed over the past twenty-five years, much also remained the same. In the (post)apartheid city much of the segregated urban fabric remained, and, sometimes, even intensified. The apartheid city structure is perpetuated by a government housing program that builds free houses for the poor in townships on the fringes of the city, inaccessible to the resources and economic opportunities the city has to offer (Turok, 2012:32–33). In providing free houses, owned by people themselves, poor families acquire a vital asset, which cannot be underestimated. At the same time, however, a huge opportunity is being missed to radically reweave the city's spatial fiber. The poor remain restricted to the same townships specifically designed for blacks during apartheid. Socio-spatial justice—mediated by equal access to the city and its opportunities—remain elusive for the majority of urban dwellers.

Since the 1990s capital shifted from the inner city to the suburbs, causing inner-city decay and the mushrooming of suburban security estates. Some say that the fastest growing neighborhoods in South Africa today are gated communities on the one hand and sprawling informal settlements on the other.[1] In some ways, these represent the pathological codependencies that keep the resource-rich comfortable, and the resource-poor trapped. In Woodlane Village, these paradoxes live side by side.

The Gauteng City-Region—home to the large metropolitan areas of Johannesburg and the City Tshwane (Pretoria) among others—has grown from 9 million to 14.7 million people in the period from 2002–18 (GCRO, 2018). This is due largely to rural-urban migration and the transnational inflow of people from other African countries. The majority of new arrivals to South African cities tend to be poor black South Africans coming from rural areas. This is evident in the growth, not only of informal settlements but of backyard dwellings, which grew by 205 percent in the Gauteng City-Region between 2001 and 2016—and today outnumber the dwellings of informal settlements (Hamman, Mkhize & Götz, 2018).

Some of the most racially integrated neighborhoods can be found among higher-end economic groups, often concentrated in newly built gated communities. There are also a few examples of traditionally poorer white neighborhoods that have become well-integrated, simply because the white residents of such neighborhoods often have limited options to relocate elsewhere. And yet, the majority of black South Africans still live in urban townships, urban informal settlements, or backyard shacks on the urban fringes, whilst the majority of white South Africans still live in secluded and segregated suburbs. We still go to separate churches for the most part, separate schools, and separate socializing spaces.

Woodlane Village is a metaphor for all of the above. It hosts migrants from several African countries as well as people seeking economic access closer to the city. What makes it unique is its location at the heart of one of the City of Tshwane's wealthiest neighborhoods. In this way it presents a challenge but also an opportunity to the city—and citizens of the city—to model a form of spatial transformation that will be radically inclusive of all people—in this case not just racially but also economically; truly equitable; whilst at the same time enhancing the quality of life for all who live in that part of the city.

---

[1] Statistics South Africa (n.d.) shows that 80.7 percent of the City of Tshwane's population lived formally and 19.3 percent informally by 2011.

SPATIAL WOUNDS—PAST AND PRESENT

Woodlane Village needs to be read against the backdrop of the apartheid city. The apartheid project was in essence a spatial project. Segregation was institutionalized and legitimized. According to often arbitrary racial classifications, people were forced to live in segregated neighborhoods. In 1958 a policy was crafted to determine the racialization of spatial arrangements in Pretoria, to be aligned to the new Group Areas Act of 1950. Certain neighborhoods, where people lived for generations, were reclassified. Neighborhoods such as Marabastad, Lady Selborne, Bantule, Kilnerton, Hercules, and others, had to be de-Africanized, and were declared white. Such segregation was not restricted to neighborhoods, but extended to schools, churches, universities, public swimming pools, and even intimate relationships. For every possible eventuality there was an (in)appropriate law.

Bulldozers tore into neighborhoods destroying physical structures such as houses, schools, and churches. At a deeper level though, communities, families, dreams, and lives were shattered. The scars of forced displacement spread across communities of color all over South Africa.

Today spatial wounds are still visible in places like Marabastad in Pretoria or District Six in Cape Town, where fifty years later gaping holes sit where once-vibrant neighborhoods dwelled together.[2] Through forced removals, legal and illegal evictions, and gentrification by entrepreneurial middle-classes, displacing the urban poor (predominantly people of color), new wounds have been inflicted since 1994.

The spatial wounds are what the eyes can see. And yet, the spatial wound is but a physical manifestation of an equally devastating psychological and spiritual wound, resurfacing today in younger generations. Some of these injuries are present in Donald's stories of urban transformations and forced relocations.

On the one hand, the ghost of apartheid is with us, haunting both poor and rich, both black and white. Theologically though, I also hold that the Spirit who hovered over the waters of the earth at the beginning, is still hovering today, over wounded cities and towns. The question is whether we will succumb to the ghost of the past, or whether we will respond to the provocations of the Spirit in the present.[3]

Woodlane Village and its surrounding gated communities concentrate socio-spatial disparity into a condensed and defined space. Provocatively, the Village runs counter to gentrification narratives where young professionals drive up property prices in dilapidated inner-city neighborhoods and, in doing so, displace generations of poorer tenants. Here, those who are resource-poor locate themselves in proximity of the city's resources, with the potential to animate a different kind of urbanism: neither urban decay eating away at the soul of neighborhoods, nor gentrification at the expense of the poor; but reurbanizing that models a creative sharing of urban land and resources, making innovative spaces that cross all kinds of barriers. It would be at the city's own peril to lose such an opportunity.

A similar provocation is seen in the suburbanization of homelessness (De Beer & Vally, 2015:63–65) in cities across South

[2] Consider Ezekiel Mphahlele's *Down Second Avenue* (1959), which describes life in Marabastad, Pretoria, prior to forced removals that destroyed this neighborhood; also *"Buckingham Palace," District Six* by Richard Rive (1986) doing the same for District Six in Cape Town, but also describing the removals itself.

[3] See De Beer (2018), *Mother Bird Hovering over the City: Space, Spirituality and a Community-based Urban Praxis*, pp. 360–363.

Africa. Instead of being able to keep the poor out of sight, the poor make places where places for them do not officially exist. Now in sight, resident associations, faith-based groups and other citizens can no longer keep conversations about homelessness and the poor out of their ordinary daily conversations.

If Woodlane Village is indeed God taking place, it could be interpreted as the hovering Spirit, prompting us to engage in new conversations about the spatiality of injustice, the humanizing of our cities, the very essence of life and death.

THE MONUMENTAL AND THE ORDINARY

In a market economy the "monumental" is prioritized over the "ordinary," and informality is often dismissed. To regenerate challenging urban places, governments and private sector actors would rather invest in mega-projects with a promise of maximized profits than invest in the challenges faced by ordinary places or people, if these show insufficient promise of financial return.

In South Africa, there are numerous examples of multibillion-rand urban revitalization projects, often in neighborhoods where the housing stock and general living conditions have deteriorated due to disinvestment. Yet very little investment is made to improve the living conditions of ordinary people, once again prioritizing the monumental.

The previous mayor of the City of Tshwane, according to the timeline shown in this book, made an attempt in 2015 to sell off the land on which Woodlane Village is situated, in breach of a court order. This was in the hope of optimizing profit on this land, which might be compromised if the legal judgment is to be honored.

If ordinary citizens do not protect the ordinary then no one else will do so. The work of affirming the ordinary requires intention and deliberate action. This is also true for retrieving the gift of the ordinary in the informal—often dismissed or misrecognized. Unless places such as Woodlane Village and its people rise up with their own agency, connected to others of solidarity, external (even global) forces will always determine their fate.

Stewart (2007:44–45) says: "Rogue intensities roam the streets of the ordinary." By way of example, Lima and Pallamin (2010:39-48) show how grassroots housing movements in São Paulo changed the urban poor from being voiceless into political subjects, forcing open crucial dialogues over the housing crisis in São Paulo. It gave rise to a counter-forum known as Forum Centro Vivo, bringing together housing movements with trade unions, student unions, churches, and NGOs to advocate housing policies "that would avoid displacing social groups victimized by real-estate development" (Lima & Pallamin, 2010:50).

It is precisely such rogue intensities that Pieterse and Simone (2013) search for in their work, *Rogue Urbanism*, to describe the nature of African cities and their evolution. Rogue intensities restlessly roam the streets of Woodlane Village, giving shape to an urbanism "from below."

INFORMALITY AND AGENCY

Too often conventional wisdom regards informality—and informal settlements in particular—as an object to be eradicated, or, at least, improved. It is perhaps in the face of this perpetual dismissal and constituted by a certain restlessness, that rogue intensities erupt from the streets of the ordinary (cf. Pieterse, 2011:1–4).

Seldom are informal settlements and their inhabitants viewed as subjects possessing wealthy reservoirs of knowledge and experience. The resilience and resistance with which informal settlement dwellers live their lives, raise their families, and carve out better futures are seldom appreciated for the assets they represent.

What apartheid planning and contemporary displacements could not destroy, even though it might have left psychological scars, is a sense of deep memory, the perpetual surprise of human tenacity in spite of suffering, and the extraordinary faith found with ordinary people in ordinary places.

Elsewhere, Bailey, De Beer, and Hankins (2018) comment on this:

> The lived spatiality, or quiet politics (cf. Hankins, 2017), practiced by backyard dwellers, shack dwellers and other (homeless) migrants, give us insight into the agency they possess, the choices they make and the reason for those choices, the spaces they choose to inhabit, and how they mediate socio-spatial relationships creatively on a daily basis.

The people of Woodlane Village, although by no means an ideal neighborhood, possess a kind of agency that leaves one in awe. The choices they make are obvious, when one comes to think of it, in pursuit of access to the city's resources and employment, in defiance of inhumane urban spatial planning favoring the wealthy few, and on the side of a better future for their children and their grandchildren. The options they exercise are done in lieu of any other equally favorable options. If the city does not extend the right of access to the city, its resources, and its city-making processes, people who have little to lose will claim such a right by where they locate themselves, even if their placemaking is deemed "illegal" by some.

MAKING LIFE; MAKING PLACE; MAKING HOME

The images and narrative accounts contained in this collection are artfully and sensitively done, with deep respect for the lives and moments that are captured. Images of Donald toiling over his sewing machine, a Sunday afternoon football match, the interior of his shack, counseling a neighbor, stoking fires for warmth, all speak of ordinary activities, seeking to make a life, to make a place, and to make a home.

Graham and Low (2009) say: "Places are made by human beings living in them, infusing them with meaning and value, through relationality." One can say that those who live in the Village have turned an empty palette into a place, "infused with meaning and value," where people meet together, pray together, play together, and even have a scuffle together on a Saturday afternoon, but life goes on.

Woodlane Village has become a place of *belonging*—albeit one that is experiencing the ongoing disruptions to neighborliness that come from high levels of transiency. It provides its residents with the opportunity for mutual hospitality. Such hospitality was not necessarily offered to them by the surrounding community. And yet, even that has started to shift with time. The "other" now gets recognized, at least by some. In time, this whole precinct might be spoken of as a place of "democratic hospitality" (Dungey, 2007:257), which opened up possibilities for a new kind of shared humanity. Such hospitality, according to Dungey, is to "recognize the Other as being here, with us, and for whom she is." Once established, it is possible to accompany each other to a new way of being human together.

Woodlane Village also offers the promise of *becoming*: people's presence in this space turns into a springboard to possible new and better futures, for them and their children. Here, together, they make life, they *become* a community, and, in their mutual struggle, they are becoming part of something much bigger, unknowingly even, connected to similar struggles across the country and, indeed, the globe. It also offers an opportunity to the broader community surrounding it, of learning how to become human together; how to open up to "the other" in a way that fosters mutuality. The apartheid city denied us this gift.

Places like Woodlane Village need to be welcomed if we are to grow in our capacity to be human.

Place-making in this instance is an act of *resistance*. Against the odds of those wishing them away, they remain, turning an empty space, overgrown by "alien vegetation," into a generative space, in which Donald, and others create, through their craft, resources for daily living.

PROPHET TO THE CITY

I deem the disruptive presence of the Woodlane Village—surrounded by high-end shopping malls, a mega-church, one of South Africa's most expensive golf estates, gated communities, and a private hospital—to be *a prophetic irruption* or *insurgency* (Perkinson, 2013: 165–198), breaking into a part of the urban landscape that traditionally disallowed the poor from habitation, except if it was to provide services or labor.

The repeated indignities bestowed on this community—both by local government and the police—are telling. Attempts by surrounding homeowner associations to secure a legal eviction of the informal settlement, which could have resulted in its eventual eradication, failed. Emotional distance, detachment, and lack of authentic relationships probably make it easy for human beings to argue the destruction of others' homes and their banishment from one's own neighborhood. At a deeper level though, could it be that "the other," represented here in Woodlane Village, is still perceived as a nonperson,[4] even if unconsciously so?

The prophet's task is to name that which is wrong, to help imagine radical alternative possibilities, and to call people to change in order for such possibilities to have a chance of being realized. It is in this sense that I consider Woodlane Village to be a prophet to the city: surfacing specific challenges; offering the possibility of new imaginations; and, should such imaginations be courageously embraced, the promise of a neighborhood displaying the foretaste of a more humane, equitable, and just city.

The presence of Woodlane Village redefines "public subjects" and "public spaces" (Lima & Pallamin, 2010:42), calling into question the stark distinctions made between formal and informal,[5] and opening possibilities for new modes of political and spatial engagement.

Firstly, it surfaces very definite challenges in a rather visible manner: the reality of ongoing spatial segregation, the resultant socioeconomic exclusion, and the vastness of inequality; the ongoing centrality of race, class, and gender in spatial production; the politics of spatial planning: who gets to participate and who is excluded; the challenge of being human together in contested spaces; and the theological question of the meaning and vocation of church amidst urban contestation.

Secondly, not only does it surface existential challenges, but it offers the real possibility to foster a daringly new and prophetic spatial imagination. It makes one wonder about a new neighborhood that will display radical inclusiveness and demonstrate viable and sustainable cohabitation: racially, economically, and generationally, but also in terms of innovative urban design that fosters ecological well-being and shared abundance.

---

4 Vuyani Vellem (2012) describes what was meant with the term "nonperson" in its use by black theologians of liberation: "Nonperson originally meant that black lives are doomed to second-class citizenship, it meant poverty in squalid conditions, and it meant ultimately being less than human."

5 In their book, *Johannesburg: The Elusive Metropolis* (2008), Mbembe and Nuttall assert: "Analytically as well as in people's daily experience, simplistic oppositions between the formal and the informal are unhelpful." Urbanity in Africa is much more complex and needs to be investigated as such.

The presence of Woodlane Village in this part of the city is provoking a reimagination of the Village itself, and how it could be integrated in sustainable and appropriate ways in this precinct, providing access to decent and affordable housing and other social, economic, and educational resources. It goes much deeper though, inviting the reimagination of 70 hectares of public land. How should public land best be stewarded in a country marked by landlessness, homelessness, and broad-based socio-economic exclusion? What would ethical urban design look like in such a contested space?

It invites the reimagination of the entire precinct, however, because what happens on one site surely affects neighboring sites and vice versa. It provokes the delightfully challenging question of how poor urban residents and residents of a wealthy golf estate could live side by side, in mutually liberating and enriching ways.

Thirdly, theologically, it invites the reimagination of the church (in its various expressions) as it is incarnate in this precinct: Can the church afford to remain neutral or is neutrality by default a theological and political position? What shape should the church take as new urban forms unfold, and will the church allow herself to be storied in conversation with prophetic irruptions from below, and in response to the hovering Spirit?

Finally, it carries the seeds—and promise—of a neighbor-hood embodying spatial healing, racial healing, humanization of relationships between people who come from vastly different backgrounds, humanization of the church, and the mediation of a very concrete sense of spatial justice and inclusion.

STORYING. AND BEING STORIED.

This collection of images represents staggering layers of overlapping stories. Every image in this book tells a story of its own. And every story will evoke different responses and emotions with those drawn into it.

Every person—woman, man, or child—living in Woodlane Village, has their own story. Just as every person living in the gated communities around the Village has their own story. The members of the church adjacent to the Village each have their own story.

The bigger story of this book is of a people trying to make a place. There is also the story of those trying to prevent them. And the story of a church—the Moreleta Park Dutch Reformed Church—and of other churches in the vicinity, grappling with the meaning of being church here. This is an unfolding story; a story that has already gone through various permutations; and still storying itself.

There is also the story, beautifully captured, of members of an African Initiated Church, worshipping with great dignity, out in the open. Another image captures members of a similar church, fervently praying on the floor of an informal structure. The caption underneath says: "We walk by faith not by sight." That conviction is etched on the faces of those kneeling. And, in some ways, etched on the face of a Village that stubbornly persists in making life against the odds.

There is the larger story too, of a people of faith, living in both the informal settlement and in the golf estate; worshipping in both the big church and out in the veld; yet, not always faithful enough to be as one.

The human rights lawyers have their own stories. Their lives intersecting with many similar sites of struggle, across the width and breadth of the country, theirs are often untold stories of unsung heroes, painstakingly fighting in the corner of those who has nobody else to fight for them.

There is the inspiring story of Denise and Colin Dredge, two ordinary people whose lives intertwined with those of Donald and many others in the Woodlane Village. The Village storied them into becoming heroes of faith for many of us—unlikely activists standing in solidarity with the people of the Village.

Or the stories of brave faith and commitment of those who pioneered the schools for children from the Village, hosted by the big church.

The story of the Woodlane Village is also the story of many, like me, who have been at arms' length: distant friends of Woodlane Village, its people, the Dredges, and others. But, strangely, ever closer drawn to the flame of hope that burns here. Because there is just this sense that there might be something here not to be missed. Coming close to the flame, one can get burnt. Or, drawing from its energy, one might have a chance to participate in fueling a new reality.

Of course, there would not be a collection of images and an accompanying narrative without the story of the photographer. His is a story of homecoming, perhaps at first glance in an unlikely place, paradoxically with people who some might regard as homeless, whilst for the people themselves, they are making home. From the images and conversations with Pieter, it became clear that they also made home for him. We are deeply indebted to Pieter de Vos for gifting us with this collection of images and the storylines undergirding it.

These images are powerful. I am convinced they would leave no story untouched, as we allow ourselves to be invited into the stories and homes of all those portrayed in this book.

This is too important a story not to be told. It might be seen as a small story of ordinary people, but—if we heed it as a prophetic irruption—it might just be one of this (post)apartheid city's most significant stories. In its simplicity it represents thousands of similar stories across the urban landscape simply trying to make life: to belong, to become, to have home. In doing so, they resist the status quo, shaping a new urbanity that has a more human face.

Thank you for extending your hospitality to us, the readers and viewers, as we are allowed into your space.

REFERENCES

Bailey, A., De Beer, S. & Hankins, K., 2018, *Dwelling as Just Faith: Migrant Housing, Precarity, and the Activities of Faith-based Organizations in Tshwane and Atlanta*, in De Beer, S. (ed), *Just Faith: Local Responses to Planetary Urbanization*, AOSIS, Cape Town.

Bergmann, S., 2008, "Making Oneself at Home in Environments of Urban Amnesia: Religion and Theology in City Space," *International Journal of Public Theology*, 2(1), 70–97.

De Beer, S., 2018, *Mother Bird Hovering over the City: Space, Spirituality and a Community-based Urban Praxis*, Unpublished PhD thesis in Town and Regional Planning, University of Pretoria, Pretoria.

De Beer, S. & Vally, R., 2015, *Pathways Out of Homelessness*, Research report, University of Pretoria, Pretoria.

De Gruben, C., 2017, *Urban Migration in Global South Cities*, published March 3, 2017, http://www.degruben.com/urban-migration-in-global-south-cities/, retrieved July 28, 2018.

Dungey, N., 2007, "The Ethics and Politics of Dwelling," *Polity*, vol. 39, no. 2, April 2007, 234–258.

Eigelaar-Meets, I., 2018, *Internal Migration in Post-apartheid South Africa: The Cases of the Western and Northern Cape*, Unpublished PhD thesis, University of Stellenbosch, Stellenbosch.

Gauteng City-Region, 2018, Gauteng City-Region, www.gcro.ac.za, retrieved August 15, 2018.

Graham, E. & Lowe, S., 2009, *What Makes a Good City? Public Theology and the Urban Church*, Darton, Longman & Todd Ltd., London.

Hamman, C., Mkhize, T. & Götz, G., 2018, *Backyard and Informal Dwellings: 2001–2016*, published February 28, 2018, http://gcro.ac.za/outputs/map-of-the-month/detail/backyard-and-informal-dwellings-2001-2016/, retrieved July 28, 2018.

Horrell, M., 1958, *Pretoria. Group Areas. Proclaimed 6 June 1958*, South African Institute for Race Relations (SAIRR), Johannesburg (retrieved from the archive of the South African Institute of Race Relations (1892–1974), which is held at the Historical Papers Research Archive at The University of the Witwatersrand in Johannesburg).

Lima, Z.R. & Pallamin, V.M., 2010, *Informal Practices in the Formal City: Housing, Disagreement and Recognition in Downtown Sao Paulo*, in Hernández, F., Kellett, P. & Allen, L.K. (eds), 2010, *Rethinking the Informal City: Critical Perspectives from Latin America*, Berghahn Books: New York & Oxford.

Mbembe, A. & Nuttall, S. (eds) 2008, "Introduction: Afropolis," in *Johannesburg: The Elusive Metropolis*, Wits University Press, Johannesburg.

Mphahlele, E., 1959, *Down Second Avenue*, Faber & Faber, London.

Parnell, S. & Pieterse, E., 2014, *Africa's Urban Revolution*, Zed Books, London & New York.

Perkinson, J. W., 2013, *Messianism Against Christology: Resistance Movements, Folk Arts, and Empire*, Palgrave Macmillan, New York.

Pieterse, E., 2011, "Introduction: Rogue Urbanisms," *Social Dynamics*, 37:1, 1-4.

Pieterse, E. & Simone, A. M. (eds), 2013, *Rogue Urbanism: Emergent African Cities*, Jacana Media & ACC Publication, Cape Town.

Rive, R., 1986, *"Buckingham Palace," District Six*, David Philip, Cape Town.

Statistics South Africa, n.d., City of Tshwane, http://www.statssa.gov.za/?page_id=1021&id=city-of-tshwane-municipality, retrieved July 25, 2018.

Turok, I., 2012, *Urbanisation and Development in South Africa: Economic Imperative, Spatial Distortions and Strategic Responses*, International Institute for Environment and Development (IIED), London.

Vellem, V., 2012, "Interlocution and Black Theology of Liberation in the 21st Century: A Reflection," *Studia Historiae Ecclesiasticae*, vol. 38, Supplement, pp. 345–360.